IN REAL TIME

by

The Amazing Kreskin

———⟨⟩———

New York

THANE & PROSE

2015

In Real Time © 2015 The Amazing Kreskin
Published by Thane & Prose, New York
All rights reserved
Book cover and book interior design by Jerry Holthouse
ISBN: 9780997079524
Printed in the U.S.A

THANE
&
PROSE

To those of you who share with me a love of the animal world;
I have a special bond—clearly we are here to share with this earth.

IN REAL TIME

FOREWORD

I've known Kreskin for many years now and have always been surprised and fascinated by all those abilities he has shown us on the various shows I have done. He always was one of the guests I loved and why shouldn't he be? Who else could be called on to stand up and perform some mental magic that you would never see again?

People have always asked me 'How does he do it?' I didn't know then and all these years later, I still don't know. All I know is, he is the only one I've ever met who could do such things.

He was on Carson many times but he did 105 TV shows with me, and has written many books—but now comes something different and very important. This, his 20th book, is a book of visions he has written about what is happening in this crazy world we live in today. He is not just predicting things, he wants to tell you what he sees in the years, the decades—and the centuries to come.

I have never met anyone like Kreskin. He is unique and brilliant and I can't wait to read his latest.

—*Regis Philbin*

MY VISION BEGINS

You are about to read my descriptions of twenty-five irrepressible visions that came to me between 2008 and 2015.

Let it be known that in my lifetime, I have never received so many mystical previews in such a small window of time. Why now? I have come to the conclusion that there is *purpose* in these transmissions; but to what end, exactly, I do not yet know.

It is my belief, however, that by drawing your attention to these transmissions, I might possibly prevent certain dire events from occurring.

Admittedly, I wondered if w hat was coming through to me could be construed as urgent warnings. Were the fates, or powers that orchestrate the pluses and minuses in our universe, becoming angry with our constant blundering, mistakes, and disregard for our planet?

A troubling question, indeed, but one in need of pursuit.

And so we embark, and I ask you to prepare yourself for the many happenings, both dark and luminous, I am about to share.

The words and feelings that follow are as they were when these events unfolded. Much has been taken from my notes written soon after the visions ended; other observations, added later, are meant to assist in providing you a broader overview of what I experienced.

It is also important to emphasize that throughout my entire life I have seen things, known things, and sensed things far beyond what any person would ever consider normal.

For the most part, I have attributed these gifts to the power of the human mind. I do not consider myself to be a modern-day Nostradamus; I neither practice astrology, nor do I read Tarot cards or rely on crystal balls.

Still, there have been many incidents, both on stage and in front of television cameras, when I was able to do what bewildered onlookers considered the impossible.

The truth? I was just as bewildered.

One such instance happened early in my career. For publicity purposes, I had made predictions of headlines that would appear the following week on the front page of a local newspaper. The predictions were then locked in a box and stored in a safe at the local bank. It was all part of an annual Founder's Day event in a small Pennsylvania town, which for them was a major happening.

Each edition leading up to my performance featured editorials anticipating whether The Amazing Kreskin could actually accomplish a feat as incredible as forecasting the four or five news stories that would be featured on the following Sunday's front page.

After all, everyone knew this was *impossible.*

Consequently, there was great anticipation when the week had finally passed. The editor of the paper, with the next morning's edition in hand, appeared on stage during my evening performance, accompanied by the mayor and president of the bank. The standing-room-only crowd offered them an enthusiastic round of applause, then leaned forward in anticipation of what my locked-up predictions would reveal. One by one, the headlines were read aloud.

Each of my predictions proved incredibly accurate, even to the most finite detail; however, one of my predicted headlines was glaringly absent from the front page.

Had The Amazing Kreskin finally been wrong?

A week earlier, I knew I needed at least one more prediction, but, frankly, nothing that appeared in my mind seemed newsworthy. Finally, in desperation, I wrote about what I had considered an unlikely happening but one that kept lingering in my subconscious. This last prediction focused on a possible crime that would take place near a theater. I figured it was probably wrong, but I was aware time was running out and I needed to get everything down on paper and submitted to the editor.

Now, here is the ironic twist to this story: even as the group on stage was discussing my missing headline, there was a commotion outside the theater. There were sirens, whistles, and the screeching of police car tires. It was loud enough to be heard by audience members, even to the balcony's last row. We were clearly in the midst of a hyper escalating emergency.

As it turned out, that emergency was exactly the crime that I had predicted, but hoped, would not happen.

Too late to make the paper's headlines.

The newspaper and the mayor later credited me for accurately predicting the robbery, though they needn't have. It was but one of hundreds of such examples of fate confirming the accuracy—and truth—behind what I do.

In fact, it is this accuracy and truth that distinguishes me, making it possible for me to reach back and defy *the impossible*.

Fortunately, these out-of-nowhere mini-miracles continue to this very day.

And as impossible as it may appear, throughout my entire life, I have been able to direct my mind so that I could see the future; conversely, many of my visions have come to me spontaneously, as I will share with you a bit later. But perhaps even more incredible, most of my visions have proved startlingly accurate; yet, I continue to maintain that I have never considered myself another Nostradamus.

Why?

At the end of the day, I am an entertainer—and I wish to remain as such. Surprised? Don't be. I have never wanted future generations to look back at me and envision Kreskin peering into a crystal ball, or staring up at the stars as they do Nostradamus. To be frank—it's just not who I am, publicly, privately, or in any form of persona.

Despite my strange abilities, which I do not thoroughly understand myself, I am very much like everyone else. Although I have very little time to partake in life's pleasures, I do like good books, and well-made movies, the theater, intelligent TV— and a good seafood dinner now and again.

I also appreciate the loyalty of my fans. You, each of you, are truly wonderful.

Though truth be told, I do not enjoy being pointed at in public, or approached by strangers asking me to predict their future. Often I am posed with questions such as: "Who is going to win the Kentucky Derby?" or "Will the home team make it into the World Series?" or "Who will win the Stanley Cup?" or even "Who will be the next Masters Champion?"

I refuse all such requests.

In fact, I go a step further: I purposely try to block these events out of my mind for two reasons; the first, is that I never want to be in a position to accidentally blurt out the response to any of these questions; the second, I simply spend too much of my time traveling to pay sufficient attention to what is happening on the sports pages.

Yes, some things are best blocked out of my mind, mostly because I believe mine is a special gift and not to be used frivolously, purposely, or indirectly to assist anyone in having a secret advantage, particularly in any endeavor where wagers can be made.

Yet, on certain occasions, I have publicly discussed some of the potential happenings my mind has envisioned. For example, as each new year approaches, beginning the day after Christmas and continuing through the first week the New Year's holiday, I am interviewed by scores of broadcasters and writers, people from Fox News, CBS, NBC and other smaller networks, all desirous of my revelations of what I see for the next 12 months. But none of these purposeful prognostications has ever rivaled the kinds of revelations that follow here.

VISION No.1

An Early Morning Jog in a Park in New Orleans

———⁂———

As a performer doing many one-nighters in various cities, I have always realized the importance of keeping myself in sound physical condition. This includes eating correctly, watching my weight and exercising as often as possible—particularly when, in addition to my usual two-hour performance, I am required to participate in a meet-and-greet session where I respond directly to questions. Such was the situation prior to appearing in one of my favorite destinations: New Orleans.

As our plane approached The Big Easy, I remembered how rain had caused substantial damage to its Superdome during Hurricane Katrina, threatening the thousands of its residents huddled inside.

It was the New Orleans rain that was again causing a problem this particular night. It forced us to keep circling until the downpour let up slightly. There was no getting away from it: we were going to be late. To make matters more stressful, I realized I also had to fulfill the scheduled social part of my appearance.

Fortunately, I had a great audience. Even though the weather and other factors pushed back the start of my show by 40 minutes, their enthusiasm resulted in several encores. The flip side was that I was on stage longer than I had anticipated and consequently, I was terribly exhausted when I finally returned to my hotel.

Nevertheless, the next morning I was still able to wake up at 5:00 a.m. re-energized and ready to tackle a jog along the pathways of a large park directly across the street. My hotel was located in the city's Garden District, which is home to many celebrities and authors. I eagerly slipped into my running shoes, and I was on my way.

Little did I know it would be one of the most memorable jogs I was to ever take.

As I passed the hotel clerk, he suggested I limit my run to the immediate area around the hotel; it seemed the attractive park nearby was a prime area for occasional assaults. However, in my typical fashion, I disregarded his warning. The park across the street seemed to beckon to me.

It was still dark, and the trees and shrubs cast ominous shadows as I made my way around a heavily wooded path; despite that, I was thinking ahead to my appearance the following day in the Midwest.

Then it happened.

Without any apparent reason, my mind went blank, something unusual for someone who is considered an expert on mind control. Within weeks of this experience I had had myself checked out by a qualified neurologist, who to my great relief, found no abnormalities. Still, my first reaction was to wonder if I was having a stroke or some kind of seizure. I was not. In fact, later I realized this was just the first of the sudden, unplanned, mysterious visions that were to visit me over the next five years. But this one was different from any of my other, less important visions—very different.

What I felt first was a slight sense of dizziness and loss of balance. There was a bench nearby, so I eased onto it and let my head fall back gently.

As my mind regained focus, what came into view was the first of the incredible visions. It was almost as if I was looking at a large movie screen.

At this point, let me be perfectly clear: what I saw, I later carefully detailed in notes back in my hotel room. I wanted no ambiguity, nor did I want the passing of time to erode my recollection of the strange events I witnessed that morning.

Permit me to emphatically reiterate again and again: I am not, nor do I profess to be, a modern-day Nostradamus. I do not speak in quatrains or in some strange distortion of the English language. I have always made a point to be clear and precise in my writings. What's more, I will not inject any interpretation of what I have seen that might be colored by my own political or religious views.

Unequivocally—this is the vision that came to me as I sat, slightly dizzy and somewhat mystified, on that New Orleans park bench. Please be warned, what I am about to reveal is disturbing, but I will describe it exactly as I saw it.

Specifically, it warned of a massive explosion that would devastate a large part of a major American city.

This explosion may be of a 9/11 magnitude or greater. Be assured, what I was seeing and hearing was as real as if I was there (which made it all the more frightening). Still, I had no idea where it was happening. Sirens were wailing. Buildings were collapsing. People were screaming. Every part of me wanted to step into this awful scene and help, but I had no physical capacity with which to do so.

It was, as I indicated, like sitting in front of a movie screen.

All I could do was desperately try to identify some sign or landmark that might provide a clue as to exactly where this was and when it was happening. No such indicators were or would be forthcoming. Sadly, I was unable to make out any local or state license plates of the ambulances coming and going. In the midst all of this havoc, in the distance, explosions continued.

I later wondered if this was a natural disaster or possibly a terrorist attack. It was hard to believe that such a vivid catastrophic vision would explode into view one moment and vanish the next, but that brief time was long enough to leave me shaken and convinced that I had actually been amidst massive chaos.

What was even more disturbing was that I could see faces: people with blood streaming from open wounds, firefighters wearing expressions of determination and desperation, police shouting into portable communicators. However, as specific and graphic as all this was, all of the street signs seemed to be blurred—or carefully censored. It was almost as if the force transmitting this vision into my mind did not want me to know where and when this was to happen.

The experience was vexing!

I emerged from this chaotic state with few clues; however, while still there, I had noticed frost coming out of rescuers' mouths and snow on the ground. Also, for some reason, the year 2018 kept resonating in my mind. A random date? Perhaps. But it was the closest contextual clue I could gather from the vision of this apocalyptic tragedy.

In the weeks that followed, I began to realize that this particular vision was actually the onset of a sequence that I detail in this book. So I asked myself, could this New Orleans vision, because it was my first, have some extra-special significance? Are we, as a nation, on the verge of some new horrific danger?

I keep hoping it is a warning of what might be instead of what will be.

Many months went by after I experienced this vision, during which time I desperately tried to re-focus my mind back on to that frightening scene to identify where and when this possible tragedy might take place. In fact, I have even tried passing my hands over maps of the United States, seeking a feeling, a vibration, or anything else that might enable me to zero in on a specific area of the country.

So far, no luck; consequently, I am left only with a nagging premonition of possible devastation—and the awful sense that this may happen in the winter of 2018. This vision has left me with a commitment to never stop seeking more information about this disturbing potential disaster.

Approximately seven weeks passed after first troubling vision. When the next one occurred—it was equally shocking.

VISION No. 2

*A Potential Massive Attack on Our Power Grids,
Knocking Out All Electricity in the United States*

———————

What I will now relate is another example of how unpredictable these visions were. They could come at any time, at any place, and under any conditions.

I was now comfortably settled into a rare two days of rest back home in New Jersey. It was early evening, and the TV was tuned to a political discussion, my preferred type of viewing.

This was supposed to be a time of relaxation, but no, a vision would appear—one that not only hit me with a vengeance, but commanded me with authority. It began with the same sense of dizziness and lack of balance I had experienced during my vision in New Orleans. But this time, I was not in a park, I was comfortable at home—then, in another country.

However, location was irrelevant. Almost immediately the picture on the TV set completely disappeared. There was an inky blackness, followed by the ceasing of operation of anything electrical: no ticking, no artificial sound of any kind. Instinctively, I reached for my cell phone, but it, too, was dead. As before, I again seemed to be a mere spectator of what was happening.

In the midst of all of this blackness, a vision of a huge industrial complex ominously emerged.

I cannot begin to describe how eerie this was. It seemed to just appear out of the darkness, almost like something in a horror film. Its many buildings were flanked by large electrical towers and enveloped in a dense, gloomy fog. I had no idea where these factories were located, but in front of each structure stood a pole displaying a foreign flag with what seemed to be Asian or Middle Eastern markings.

Fortunately, there seemed to be nothing to prevent me from entering through the doors of the structures. Accordingly, I wandered from building to building; inside were hundreds of workers working at what appeared to be endless rows of computers.

Suddenly, red flags were flashing in my head. Again and again. Over and over. Instinctively, I realized: this was an enemy.

In effect, I was being told that what I was viewing represented a serious potential danger to the United States and possibly all of the free world.

One thought seemed to dominate my thinking: was I witnessing preparations for a future attempt to knock out the free world's power grid? (I had no idea why this seemed to be the prominent thought in my mind, but I had absolutely no doubt that what I was viewing presented an acute danger.) Fortunately, on the wall, I could clearly observe a calendar; in fact, many calendars. While I could not see a day, I could make out the year: 2016.

After what felt like an eternity, the darkness disappeared and all seemed to return to normal. I found myself still sitting in my lounge chair. The lights and everything dependent on electricity were working with no difficulty. Furthermore, there was no indication that anything had interfered with their operation. In fact, the same news program was still in progress. Again, no more than two or three minutes had passed.

Still, I called down to several friends, including a staff member and my road manager on the floor below. All of them insisted that nothing unusual had occurred.

The significance of this vision was clear to me: in the fall of 2016, we may be in serious danger of a massive attack on the power grids of this nation—and possibly the world.

At this point, you may wonder if the things I have seen and continue to see are imminent. My instinctive response is a hopeful "No."

Why? Because, as I explained earlier, I believe the strange and mysterious forces that have sent me these visions are paradoxically intending me to *prevent* them.

Yet, you need to know that several times in the past I have had similar experiences with prophecy that were not necessarily visions, but just sudden, spontaneous predictions. Sadly (and one of the major factors behind my determination to understand my current visions), several of these came true.

The first was on January 1, 2001. Note the date. I had been invited by a TV network to offer my prophecies for the coming new year. Everyone was in a festive holiday mood, and I was shaking hands in my usual robust manner.

Soon after the pleasantries, I found myself slipping comfortably into the early stages of describing what the next 12 months might bring.

Then it happened again: out of nowhere, I blurted out that I saw two airliners crashing on September 11th. It was totally out of context to anything I had been describing, but the words sprang forth anyway. At the time, no one got too upset; however, later, on September 11th, many, of course, did.

In fact, the prediction was brought to the attention of a member of the CIA and two agents of the FBI. Needless to say, they were profoundly interested in what enabled me to make that prediction. As you might expect, these chaps had neither patience nor understanding of the supernatural. Nevertheless, after several hours, they concluded that I did not have any advance information. It was just me, making another accurate prediction—albeit one of horror and destruction, and one that privately devastated me to see it come to life.

In my lifetime, I will never recover from my sadness for America, the firefighters and officers who lost their lives, or for the innocent victims of that day.

The next strange happening on live national TV came when, as a result of my popularity in Canada, I had been requested to predict who would be elected the next Canadian Prime Minister. I had become fairly well known there because of my successful show originating in Montreal decades ago.

At the time, Paul Martin Jr. was running against Stephen Harper. Inasmuch as Canadian presidential campaigns are much shorter than those in the U.S., I made my prediction approximately two months before the election. It was stored in a locked box and kept hidden until the appropriate time.

As it turned out, my sealed prediction had caused enough enthusiasm for one of the Canadian television networks to fly me up north to be on hand when the final votes were to be tabulated.

When the locked box was opened, the morning following the election, it revealed that I had made the accurate choice of Stephen Harper. However, in the midst of the congratulations, pats on the back and high praise, I blurted out that the new administration would collapse within 14 months and the Prime Minister would not be reelected.

Later, during an intermission, I made a point of apologizing to the director. To my surprise, not only was he not angry but was clearly pleased, as his switchboard had lit up with calls from people all over the country.

I had forgotten about this incident until some months later when I returned home: awaiting me were 84 cell phone messages. All informing me that the Martin government had just collapsed and that it seems my prediction of its demise had been accurate within 5 days.

VISION No. 3

A Major Hurricane Unlike Any in The Last 50 Years Hits New York City

———————

This prediction came to me at just about the time meteorologists were eyeing the start of the 2012 hurricane season. I had completed two performances in neighboring states in the Southwest, and upon returning to my hotel I immediately fell into a much-needed deep sleep.

It didn't last long.

At approximately 3:00 a.m., I awoke suddenly to a vision of a monster storm hitting the Northeast coast of the United States. I could hear it. I could see it. There was absolutely no ambiguity to what I was viewing.

Additionally, the date was clear: it would strike in the late summer of 2018. Unfortunately, what I was witnessing was a storm like no other. This one was to be a potential horror.

Within this awful vision, I could plainly make out Bedloe's Island, home of the Statue of Liberty, with water halfway up its base. Other islands, like Ellis and Governors, were also inundated from torrential non-stop downpours that eliminated their land surfaces from sight. In the distance, I could see the skyline of the city.

Its shoreline had literally disappeared.

Later, when reviewing my notes, I wondered if 2012's Hurricane Sandy had been a preview of what was to come. Actually, I considered Sandy to be the "Mother of all Hurricanes." Her October arrival erased any lingering doubt about whether the Big Apple was immune to the ravages of a Category 4 or 5 killer storm.

That unfriendly lady went on to blow New York Harbor up onto the streets of the downtown financial center and into its subway and other transit systems, while eliminating power to 90 percent of the tri-state area. On Staten Island, Long Island and much of the New Jersey shore, its damaging sting was felt even more profoundly.

Unfortunately, Sandy may seem like a flower girl in comparison to what this new storm I envisioned may deliver to the same area in 2018.

So what to do? Not much, other than hope I am wrong (which, incidentally, I am not in any way ashamed to share with you that I have been known to be from time to time). But one thing is for sure—I would make sure the public emergency services in New York City are ready with full crews on standby, food supplies are stashed, evacuation centers staffed, and escape routes memorized.

Additionally, I would make certain that, upon notice of any "named" storm on a trajectory to hit the area, to make sure to have a full tank of gas, plenty of batteries, prescriptions filled, and a "fall-back" place in which to seek shelter.

As I have noted, there are occasions when I am wrong; in fact, more instances than I like to admit.

A fast example is the nine times out of 6,000-plus performances that I failed to find my check, hidden by a member of the audience, which is an important part of my stage performances. But, needless to say, not a bad batting average.

Yet, in an odd way, I welcome such happenings—as long as they remain few and far between. Why?

Because even though I make my living being perceived as a wielder of miracles, it's good to be reassured that I am still just a mere mortal. Certainly, if we were living back in the days of Salem, I would have been executed for being a witch.

My next prediction came soon after my vision regarding New York's upcoming monster hurricane.

VISION NO. 4

The Mystery of Amelia Earhart May Finally Be Solved

For years, I have studied all of the leads that present-day researchers have uncovered regarding Amelia Earhart's disappearance. Some were very promising, others were obviously false, so when a stunning flash vision came to me late in 2012, it captured my attention as few others have because it may have finally ended the 76-year-old mystery of the aviatrix's fate.

What I saw was a modern-day Japanese official standing in front of hundreds of reporters and photographers, making three important admissions:

1. that Amelia Earhart had been found alive on Howland Island in 1937;
2. that she had been taken into protective custody by the Empire of Japan; and
3. that she was treated well and died of an unspecified illness in 1944. He did not identify the exact location of her demise.

Unfortunately, this vision was in the form of an undated news conference. Also, it came and went so fast that I was not able to determine whether his announcement was followed by a customary question-and-answer period.

The only additional piece of information I can add is that the official was not wearing military garb. He was dressed in the kind of formal clothing usually worn by members of the Japanese government. That was the whole context of what I saw.

Nevertheless, it may very well fit with the latest clues turned up by her searchers. The most interesting of these was a freckle treatment cream jar found on Howland Island (one of Earhart's most pronounced features was highly visible freckles). Interestingly, numerous sonar pings registered off Howland's shore by state-of-the-art electronics that had not been available years earlier. Furthermore, the search team announced that the pings indicated they might well have come from an aircraft the size and shape of Earhart's.

My educated guess is that after her capture, she and navigator Fred Noonan were extensively questioned (hopefully not tortured) as to the specific reason for their flying close to Japanese-controlled islands. There were rumors that she had been requested by the U.S. government to take pictures of these islands to determine whether they were being prepared for war. After her disappearance, the United States rigorously refuted such accusations. My feeling (and this was in no way based on any additional visions) is that she and navigator Noonan were probably taken back to Japan, because Amelia was an expert on contemporary aviation construction and Noonan on avionics (both areas in which a nation preparing for war would be very much interested). As for her passing from some unspecified illness, it is very possible. But one thing for certain is that the Japanese in 1937 were not interested in any incident that would further weaken their relations with the U.S.

Every effort would have been made to keep Earhart and Noonan's capture a secret. Indeed, long after the war ended, the Empire of Japan would have desired even more so to maintain that secrecy; they wanted no barrier to their excellent relations with the country that defeated them (and later helped rebuild their nation into one of the world's great economic powers).

To this end, I also suspect that the Japanese planted pieces of evidence to make it appear that Earhart and Noonan died on Howland Island: bits of shoes, slivers of metal, etc.

Hopefully, the announcement I saw in my vision will come soon enough in the future that further pieces to this fascinating puzzle will fall into place.

Speaking of puzzles, my next revelation indicates that another enigma is about to be resolved.

VISION No. 5

The Pope Declares There is Alien Life in Outer Space

This may be the most important pronouncement of our time.

Certainly, hundreds of investigative groups have exhaustively explored every facet of this question. They have traveled to the most remote parts of the world, pored through thousands of pages of eyewitness accounts, sued for the release of government files, risked arrest for trespassing on off-limits bases, and interviewed numerous pilots and astronauts. Yet they still do not have the necessary "smoking gun."

That is why this next startling revelation was so profound.

It came shortly after watching news coverage of Pope Francis being ordained in March 2013. Perhaps that set the stage for what was to come.

I had been sitting at an airport gate waiting for a flight to Ohio and felt rather fatigued. I usually employ certain mind control techniques that enable me to perform at a high level even when exhausted, but I had just completed two stage appearances in different cities and admittedly was now on the verge of dozing off. So, in retrospect, it would have been understandable if I had slipped into a light sleep. However, what I actually slipped into was something substantially different.

I have no idea how much time passed when all of a sudden, I found myself staring at the TV screen above my seat. Everyone around me appeared to be in a state of suspended animation. The only movement in the vicinity was that of my own head looking upward.

What I saw was Pope Francis sitting in a large hall surrounded by cardinals, personal staff and many members of the press. In front of him was a small table containing numerous documents. What the pontiff was saying was astounding.

He was talking about alien life in outer space.

Up to now, this was a topic the Vatican had gone out of its way to avoid. But not now. Incredibly, he was saying (and I had to listen carefully to his interpreter) that he no longer had doubts that the heavens above are occupied by aliens with intelligence equal to or surpassing that of our own, and that it was perfectly reasonable to assume that these beings may have evolved even further.

Next came the most amazing part of his pronouncement: he expressed a desire to see them learn more about our ways and possibly even become Christians, and then went on to indicate that sometime soon he would reveal certain information collected by the Vatican through the centuries that would provide additional proof to substantiate his determination that aliens were real.

It was at that point that I was snapped back to where I was supposed to be. My watch indicated that only a few minutes had passed. In the distance, I heard my flight number being called. Almost like a robot, I boarded the plane. But for the next 96 minutes, my mind was on full throttle.

Did what I thought I saw really occur? The Pope's last few words resonated in my head. When would that "sometime soon" be? Would he reveal this certain information and additional proof that would validate his pronouncement that aliens were real?

I wondered what kind of proof this might be. I knew that words like this must have been carefully thought out before they were stated in front of the world's media. Consequently, I must conclude that he is ready to present the proof the world has been waiting for.

Incidentally, in the question-and-answer periods following my stage performances, I have often been asked about UFOs and aliens. My consistent reply has never changed: I tell all who ask such questions that while I have yet to come across an abduction story that I felt was real, I nevertheless am firmly convinced that there is life in outer space.

I then ask the audience, "How can we as people dare to be so egotistical to believe in a universe packed with millions of other solar systems and billions of planets and yet feel that we are the only intelligent life in the universe?" Usually, there is no reply.

Oh, yes one thing more: would it not be frightening to think that *we* represent the highest level of intelligent life in the universe?

It is interesting to note that in recent years the United States government finally confirmed that Area 51 actually does exist. For years, residents living within 20 miles of the site have consistently reported seeing strange lights and saucer-shaped objects in the sky. While these sightings had been experienced by fairly reliable witnesses, including police officers and pilots, the government has neither officially investigated these sightings nor acknowledged that there even was an Area 51.

As various incarnations of stealth aircraft made their debut over the years, it was hardly a secret that these state-of-the-art aircraft were tested in the secret location. Consequently, no one was shocked at the government's announcement that Area 51 existed.

For years, I have quietly investigated this intriguing piece of land 85 miles north of Las Vegas. Fortunately, I play numerous engagements in Sin City's most prestigious hotels, and this allows me time in the early mornings to rent a car and drive north toward Nellis Air Force Base, which is very close to this tightly guarded area.

My many trips there have absolutely convinced me that Unidentified Flying Objects do exist. Probably most of the ones I have personally seen were our very own fabrications, but that does not eliminate the possibility that other craft, perhaps from the far reaches of the solar system, may also have been flitting about, observing the comings and goings at this facility.

During my own personal investigations, I have talked with highly reliable men and women, including some who actually worked on the base (with the condition that their identities never be revealed), who insisted that our government had recovered a crashed saucer and has for several years been in the process of reverse-engineering its various flight and avionics systems.

Furthermore, they made maximum use of contributions by German scientists taken into custody in the latter stages of World War II. According to my sources, it is they who were major players in the development of stealth technology.

Upon learning this, I wanted to go even further by attempting (on several occasions) to project my mind behind and within whatever hangars, hidden tunnels, or other buildings that might keep such an operation a good distance away from roving eyes, cameras, and flyovers, but their security methods are sufficient to guard our eyes, and my mystical abilities, from seeing whatever it is they do not want outsiders to see.

I will conclude with a prediction that by the year 2017, the government will, once and for all, release its files on the crash at Roswell.

THE BRIGHT SIDE

At this point, let me assure you, many of my sudden "transitions into future experiences" were not all negative. Yes, there was a dark side, but there has also been a bright side. In fact, my life has been full of bright sides.

I remember checking in for a flight at New York's Kennedy Airport several years ago. The airline representative was routinely confirming my reservation and flight time at the gate. For no particular reason, I turned around and stared at a young women sitting on a bench. She had a young child next to her. I had no idea why I was doing this—I just kept staring.

I could see her clothes seemed well worn, and so did those of the youngster. Her face appeared sad. I knew instinctively that this was a woman with substantial problems. My concentration was broken when the airline representative handed my validated tickets back to me.

As I walked away, I stopped, turned around and went back to the young woman and her child sitting on the bench.

I immediately apologized for my staring and introduced myself as Mr. Kreskin; it was a good thing I left off the word "Amazing," because there was absolutely no reaction to the name Kreskin. It had no meaning to her whatsoever. Consequently, for a full 10 seconds, there was dead silence. The truth was, I did not know what I was supposed to say. Yes, the renowned mind of Kreskin was actually blank.

But not for long. An older man sitting on the reverse side of her bench turned around, pointing to me, and said, "I know you. You're The Amazing Kreskin!" With that comment, two other nearby travelers reached over to shake my hand. This obviously was enough to convince the young woman that I was not some evil old man looking for an easy pickup. In fact, she now smiled at me. I asked her name, and almost before she answered, I knew it was Regina.

I told her that I felt she was troubled and perhaps I could help. Frankly, at that point, I did not know how, but I suggested that she and her youngster accompany me to a refreshment area nearby so that we could talk privately. She nodded and took the hand of her child, and we relocated ourselves away from prying ears.

It took a few moments for her to get comfortable. She said, "People around us seemed to know you. Are you somebody famous?" I told her that I am an entertainer whom they may have read about or seen on TV. She then seemed embarrassed that she had never heard of me and apologized. Noting her discomfort, I immediately said that there are many who have never heard of me. We chatted for a few minutes, and then she broke down in tears. She told me that she had received a telegram stating that her husband was reported missing overseas. He had been stationed in Iraq and it had been weeks since she heard from him. Now, desperate and unsure of her future, she was heading to her mother's home in Seattle.

Then one of those "flash visions" occurred. Suddenly, somehow, I knew her husband was safe and would return. I looked her in the eye and told her not to worry, that he would come back. We then said our goodbyes and went our separate ways.

I had all but forgotten that incident until a few weeks later, when I was watching the morning news. The program featured a wounded but recovering soldier returning from overseas and being greeted by his wife and child. Yes, it was Regina, now smiling and happy. I had little doubt that I was meant to meet her that day at JFK.

As I indicated earlier, there have been many positive happenings and good things I have been able to be part of due to these strange abilities of mine.

But there are also visions that demand priority treatment. These are the happenings with the greatest potential impact on our country, visions that must be revealed as soon as possible.

And to reiterate, that is why I consider this book of utmost importance not only for our country—but for our world.

Naturally, you may wonder, do Kreskin's visions always turn out as he describes them? The answer is a resounding: no.

Thank the Lord.

I am relieved when a tragedy I predict fails to materialize. In fact, I am quite okay with my detractors pointing to my inaccurate predictions. I only hope I am wrong about the negative visions I describe in this book; if I am, not only will I be okay with my critics, I'll welcome them with open arms.

This raises the question: if there is a chance some of them may never occur, why should you, as a reader, take notice of what I am telling you now?

The answer is simple. Because I have been right too many times not to take all of these visions under serious consideration. It is with urgency that I had to make them known to anyone and everyone—immediately.

Consequently, the preparation for this book had to be as careful and as detailed as I could make it. I have rigorously reviewed my notes covering everything within these pages and earlier revelations. In doing so, one entry in particular caught my attention. It was dated July 16, 1996. I had dutifully made a notation that I was getting constant impressions telling me that Americans would be shot the following night.

Actually (and sadly), Americans were being shot all over the world, so I did not know where to go or what to do with my vision. It was disturbing, to say the least. But, there was no further information coming through that would allow me to warn these unfortunate Americans, whomever they might be. So it just became another entry amidst my notes.

Two days later, on the morning of July 18, I was stunned when I learned that Americans had indeed been gunned down the night before. Unfortunately, they had been passengers on an airliner that was blasted out of our skies.

It was TWA Flight 800 bound for Paris.

Initial reports told of people on Long Island's beaches observing streaks of light streaming skyward as the huge plane soared overhead. I had little doubt that what they were probably witnessing were trails from shoulder-launched missiles.

Of course, the government wanted no part of any speculation that this could possibly be a terrorist attack. Bill Clinton was too astute a politician to commit America to any kind of conflict. Consequently, they denied it vehemently and subsequent administrations continue to deny it to this very day.

Over the years, more expert witnesses and evidence have come to light that support the likelihood that this was indeed a terrorist attack. So much so that a fairly convincing documentary on the tragedy left few believing the original story that an internal electrical explosion caused the crash.

VISION No. 6

Drug-related Violence Results in the Deaths of Several Americans in Cancún and Other Mexican Resort Destinations

What probably triggered this next vision were private conversations I had with a high-level border patrol agent after a performance in Phoenix, Arizona. He was a friend of the theater owner and someone who truly had his finger on the pulse of what was going on south of the U.S. border.

I could easily see he was not comfortable to be seen sitting in a hotel lobby talking to The Amazing Kreskin. Perfectly understandable: the rampant killings and kidnappings in Mexico were now overflowing into the streets of Arizona and Texas to such a degree that no life, regardless of position or uniform, was sacred to these drug lords.

Consequently, I asked the concierge to reserve a private room in the back of the restaurant. That way, the two of us could talk privately while dining.

Later, over a cup of strong coffee, he began telling me chilling stories of the internal drug war. His main emphasis was that human lives meant nothing to the leaders of the drug lords who ran the cartels. They saw themselves as businessmen and were willing to do anything to protect the constant flow of cash, and in fact were even ready to inflict serious damage to the tourist industry that was the lifeblood of Mexico.

He pointed out that in April of 2013, seven people were found dead in the tourist resort of Cancún. Six were strangled, and one was decapitated. Clearly, the drug lords were sending a message that they would tolerate no police or military interference. He also pointed out that in a separate incident in the same resort city, the body of a man was found gagged, bound and wrapped in sheets.

Fear and intimidation were the greatest weapons of these cartel killers. They certainly knew how to use it. In total, more than 70,000 men, women and children had been killed in drug-related violence.

We ended the night with his requesting an autographed picture made out to his wife. In doing so, he added a somber thought. "Kreskin," he said, "every morning when I leave, she wonders if I will return from patrolling the border between Arizona and Mexico. I have to be honest, I often wonder the same thing. My friend, this is a real war."

The next morning, I still felt tired. I had underestimated the power of the strong coffee; it had deprived me of hours of necessary sleep. Nevertheless, I completed my early a.m. jog, which in Arizona is always wise to do before the full heat of the desert sends temperatures soaring.

When I returned, I opted for a light breakfast followed by a rest in a comfortable lounge chair in front of the hotel's Olympic-sized swimming pool. Sounds perfect, right?

Wrong. Soon after, I drifted into what was either the beginning of a prophetic vision or a terrible nightmare. Or possibly both.

This vision took me to the edge of a beach. At first, I had no idea where I was. But across the main thoroughfare was a sign, which indicated I was now in Puerto Vallarta.

As events unfolded, I soon realized this was to be a far cry from the idyllic Puerto Vallarta I had heard so much about. Why?

Because all around me people were shouting, screaming, and actually crying. It was a horrific scene, even though I was physically immune to what was taking place. I watched in disbelief as men, women and children raced into the water to escape a steady stream of bullets. They were coming from a group of vehicles.

Some of the vehicles appeared to have camouflage markings—the kinds of cars you would expect the government to deploy. But these were not mere soldiers inside; the mission of the occupants seemed to be to kill and injure as many innocent tourists as possible.

There must have been at least 30 such vehicles. Several drove right onto the beach, firing randomly at innocent sun bathers. In several instances, the cars stopped, and their occupants jumped out and physically stabbed civilians. As in the first vision described in this book, I was powerless to intervene. I was just an observer to massive carnage. What I was witnessing was savage horror.

I do not know how much time passed, but finally the attacks stopped. The vehicles pulled away, and almost on cue, the local police arrived. Later, when I "awoke," my mind retained several important pieces of information. I do not know how I came to be aware of what I knew, but it was there, flashing in my subconscious. The first was that there were a total of 73 casualties. The second was that among this number, eight were Americans. The third was the month and year.

It was April 2016.

I hope this becomes a Kreskin vision that does not come true, but I have to admit, this one was among the most realistic and disturbing I have ever experienced, particularly when you consider how many people must have been paid off on all levels to enable this kind of hateful act to occur.

Fortunately, my next destination provided a complete change of scene: Las Vegas. I had rented a car and driven all the way though Arizona, over the bridge spanning the Colorado River, past Laughlin and the numerous small desert towns heading north.

My memories of Sin City go all the way back to the days before players' cards, points and special promotions—to a time when the only way you obtained a comp was to give the house the benefit of your continuous action. If you did that, you got free rooms, women, meals, shows and top-shelf liquor.

Over the years, I played many gigs in Glitter Gulch. In the process, I got to know most of the leading headliners; I had met everyone from Sammy Davis Jr. and Redd Foxx to the many hundreds of stars who followed.

Much of this nostalgia entered my mind as I started to drive up the strip. Soon I was surrounded by a massive panorama of color, lights, motion and action. I was more convinced than ever that whether you were a gambler or not, visiting Las Vegas should be on everyone's bucket list. Today's Las Vegas is so much more than just a place to risk your money or retreat for a much-needed weekend fling. In truth, it is a garish, blazing, in-your-face opportunity for freedom to do your thing—to enjoy it—and then to leave it behind in the dust of the desert when you depart.

Keep in mind, for Las Vegas to have achieved such an aura of defiant independence, it has to possess a magical "something" evident almost upon arrival. And it does.

This "something" has been described as analogous to a non-stop New Year's Eve celebration or possibly a party overflowing from the casinos onto the streets. No other place in the whole wide world conveys such a feeling. Not Dubai. Not Macau. Not Singapore. Not Atlantic City.

In fact, I am glad I made Las Vegas' acquaintance back in the early 60s. It was then that I had one of my sudden flash visions pertaining to the town. It was incredibly prophetic, and as clear to me today as when it happened over 40 years ago.

1964 was a time when the town's first really flamboyant hotels were starting to capture the attention of America. Big corporations had wrested control over the town from the mob, and with their huge advertising budgets were trying hard to make Las Vegas break through as a leading destination for vacations, even for families.

I remember during a meet-and-greet session following one of my performances, being asked the specific question that probably was the catalyst for the prophetic flash vision mentioned below.

It was posed by a young woman, and when she asked it, the answer actually seemed relatively simple. At least that is what I thought. All she wanted to know was what might Las Vegas be like in the year 2000?

Why the year 2000? Because that marked the start of the new century. *The new millennium.* An event hardly lost on the media. And even though at the time it was still a generous 36 years away, its approach had begun to capture an increasing amount of nation-wide attention with stories, interviews, science fiction movies, and the like.

More and more, readers and viewers were starting to wonder what the millennium's debut might *really* be like. Therefore, such a question posed to the world's most respected mentalist seemed perfectly reasonable, and consequently, I wanted to answer it as accurately as I possibly could.

As it turned out, her question was like a launch pad for my mind to start probing into the future. Once again, I was starting to experience another of the flash visions that were rapidly becoming commonplace in my life. The audience could see that I was beginning to stare aimlessly. It was obvious that something very strange was happening.

I do not know how long I stood there, trying to maintain my composure. Someone in the wings noticed I was having some kind of difficulty and quickly brought me a glass of cold water. It required a mere few sips for it to bring me back.

When my head cleared, I realized I had experienced an incredible peek into this fabulous town's future. As a result, I realized Las Vegas was to become even more fantastical.

One thing was certain, the place to which I had been mentally "transported" was definitely not the Las Vegas of 1964. What I had seen was so unbelievable, so unlikely, so off the wall that I hesitated in relaying all I had envisioned to the audience. And perhaps I really should have said nothing and kept it to myself.

Yet there were fans, admirers, and tourists who had paid a substantial amount of money to witness the demonstrations of the power of my mind, which were to include any pertinent predictions I might make, unexpected or otherwise.

Accordingly, I felt duty-bound to reveal the entirety of what I saw. Not surprisingly, there were those in the showroom who began to snicker. That is how far out and near impossible my descriptions of this vision must have appeared to them. Why?

Because it became obvious that I was no longer talking about Las Vegas in 1964. Instead, I was now painting a word picture of a far-different gambling capital.

What I was describing was not one, but a collection of world-famous tourist destinations. Somehow all to be here, in Las Vegas. Furthermore, it was almost as if each location was an exact replica of our planet's most amazing sights. Little did I know that what I was envisioning was destined for sometime in the mid-2000s, and that each incredible destination was both a hotel and a fabulous casino.

Keep in mind, I was standing on a stage in 1964, and I was continuing to peer into a Las Vegas yet to be. As far as I was concerned, these visions were not only real—they were crystal clear. I could see every glittering sign, every fabulous entertainer's name, every advertised revue, and every show time.

I found myself detailing how these magnificent edifices lined both sides of the Strip as far as the eye could see. I described an Egyptian pyramid on one side and the Eiffel Tower on the other. I told of Italian palaces with dancing waters. I mentioned a scaled-down recreation of the skyline of New York City.

I even described colorful gondolas sailing around the perimeters of a classic Roman palazzo, pushed along by tenors singing romantic refrains.

And here is the part that really provoked laughter: I told the audience that directly across the Strip I not only could see an exploding volcano shooting flames skyward, but alongside were pirate ships battling in an artificial lagoon.

As you now know, all of those predictions came true. What I saw was the Las Vegas of today.

Admittedly, even I had some doubts that what I had envisioned would ever really come to pass. But it did. And needless to say, as the years went by, I was to take great satisfaction watching this miraculous transition transpire.

Later that evening, after my show was over, I agreed to be interviewed by a local newspaper reporter. NOTE: Rather than reveal her real name, I will just call her Jane.

By her tone and demeanor, I sensed she might be one of those determined skeptics who found my visions to be somewhat off the wall and that she might be predisposed to write a story that in reality would be a "hatchet job."

Accordingly, her first question was whether I was embarrassed by the audience's laughter. Her second was whether I truly believed that the recently rebuilt Las Vegas (of what was then mid-1964) would or could be replaced with anything as wild as what I had described.

My answer to her first question was "No."

My answer to her second question was that my belief in the accuracy of my visions was not important; I am merely an observer to the things I see. Naturally, I hope the good ones come true and the bad ones do not.

With that, she looked me in the eye and said, "Ok, Mr. Kreskin, make another prediction about Las Vegas right now, and I promise I won't laugh."

While I normally always refuse challenges to make on-the-spot prediction, I did not this time. Instead, I looked Jane in the eye and told her that she might want to report this additional prediction in her paper.

What I told her was that a then-popular Middle Eastern-themed hotel would eventually be replaced by a new resort-casino catering to a younger, more hip generation of gamblers. She asked me what it would be called. I closed my eyes and concentrated harder. And then I saw part of its name: It would have the word "planet" in its title.

She smiled and said, "Mr. Kreskin, I know you've had great success with many of your predictions, but I think the ones I heard today are highly unlikely."

As I now look back, I regret Jane did not go with my predictions. If so, she probably would have been considered a journalistic prophet.

But that was not the only opportunity I wanted to give her. By now, her laughter was replaced by a sarcastic smile. I told this young reporter I was going to provide an additional piece of important information that was not be opened until the year 1994. At that time, it might change her mind as to my ability to predict the future.

I kept my message hidden as I wrote it down on a slip of paper, put it in an envelope and sealed it. I then told her to write her name across the flap. That way, there was no means by which it could be opened without evidence it had been tampered with. I promised her that I would mail this very same envelope back to her in 30 years so that she could finally read its contents. She began to laugh again and said she hoped we both would be alive in 1994.

In case you were wondering what I wrote on that slip of paper that day exclusively for her (keep in mind, the year was 1964), it was as follows (in my actual words):

"In accordance with the vision I described during my performance, wherein I told of startling casino properties unlike any now in Las Vegas (or in any other gambling venue in the world), I predict even more of the same -- all built on land south of Caesar's Palace on Las Vegas Boulevard. These additional complexes will further usher Las Vegas into a whole new age of spectacular resort venues."

Signed, The Amazing Kreskin

(NOTE: Thirty years later, I did send the sealed envelope back unopened. It was addressed to her, in care of the newspaper for which she worked. I have no idea whether she ever got to read it or not. I truly hope so.)

In the decades that followed, in addition to the unbelievable resorts I envisioned that day back in 1964, Mandalay Bay was constructed—as was the Monte Carlo, The Cosmopolitan, the Aria, the MGM Grand, the South Point and the M Resort.

VISION No. 7

The Creation of the World's Most Incredible Hotel and Casino

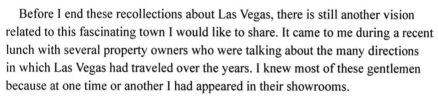

Before I end these recollections about Las Vegas, there is still another vision related to this fascinating town I would like to share. It came to me during a recent lunch with several property owners who were talking about the many directions in which Las Vegas had traveled over the years. I knew most of these gentlemen because at one time or another I had appeared in their showrooms.

The subject of the town's direction always spiked interest among all three owners because they each had their own theories as to what would be the next trend in Las Vegas' future, since they were always seeking ways to attract the "right" audience to fill their rooms, restaurants, nightclubs and entertainment venues, and, of course, keep their gaming tables and machines fully occupied.

(NOTE: It was a much-publicized fact that the town had pretty much lost its sense of direction during the last 20 years; from 1995 to 2015, it had gone from a traditional gambling destination with mass appeal, to a family vacation spot with tons of attractions for the kids, and most recently to a "let it all hang out" kind of gathering place for the 25 to 50 crowd.)

I suspected they were hoping that The Amazing Kreskin would come up with a prediction and tell them what they needed to know. I decided that I would just observe and listen; after all, the conversation was fascinating. Few others would have such an opportunity to be among such a renowned and respected group of gambling resort owners, so I decided to sit back and enjoy the fascinating banter of these gentlemen.

However, as usual, Kreskin PROPOSES and GOD DISPOSES. I never had the chance to do the relaxing I hoped for. Far from it.

Instead, I found myself suddenly gazing at a virtual dream casino edifice almost beyond man's imagination to create. I could see it completely constructed, with people going in and out, and cars driving up to its grand entrance.

It took those at my table mere seconds to realize that I was in the midst of one of my rare revelations. Once again, I was staring straight ahead. And what I was seeing was as clear as a bell.

It was the tallest hotel/casino ever built. I later instinctively realized it would tower over the highest structures in Dubai, Macau or any other place in the world. It was immense. The building I was peering at was aglow with lights caressing a dazzling mixture of glass, steel and color unlike anything you could possibly imagine. Undoubtedly, this was now to be the most fabulous showplace for a town that never hesitated to grow bigger, bolder and more alluring.

Upon my return to a semblance of normalcy, I spent a full hour describing the stunning lobby, the casino (which stretched farther than two football fields), the incredible views it provided, and the various shops and famous restaurants that would adorn its lobby.

The first reaction to my revelation was honest-to-goodness, jaw-dropping silence. But within seconds, questions flew across the table.

Each of these prominent casino owners wondered whether one of them was going to be involved in the project. Almost in unison, they asked me if I saw a name in my vision; also, they specifically wanted to know when and where it would be constructed.

I then decided to not be precise, because these casino magnates represented some of the shrewdest investors in the business. I had no intention of giving further information that might provide any one of them with an unfair advantage, as it is always my practice to avoid providing unfair advantages.

In truth, I was able to see the exact spot where this incredible complex was to be erected. And yes, I had sensed one of them definitely would be involved; however, I never indicated that I knew.

In case you are wondering when this magnificent edifice should be open for business, it will be in the spring of 2019.

And one thing more: the phrase "ation" will be in its name.

WHY NOW

At this point, one may wonder why I have not reported all or some of these visions earlier. That is fair to ask.

My best answer is that inwardly, I was trying to reach a decision as to whether this was information I really wanted the world to know. Some of it, as you have already noticed, and as you will continue to notice, is quite troubling. This is not at all my purpose. I do not take pleasure in scaring people.

But, as I have indicated, I do not know why I, of all people, have been given this strange, unexpected, out-of-nowhere insight into events yet to happen. I can only hope (and I have said this before) that by my knowing of them and describing what I have "seen," some or all of the negative happenings can either be forestalled or avoided.

Again, this is why this book has been written.

I guess it comes down to that old cliché: forewarned is forearmed. Perhaps this is what made me wonder whether my next important vision was forewarning me of something dire.

VISION No. 8

Control of Our Minds Will No Longer Be Our Own

Probably the most important factor in maintaining my reputation as a foremost mentalist has been my ability to demonstrate incredible examples of mind power, night after night. Not only have I been able to randomly choose members of the audience and "command" them to do things they never would have imagined doing in front of hundreds of people, but I could read their thoughts, as well.

The combination of these two abilities enables me to not only to produce a lot of good-natured entertainment, but also to perform feats that many would consider impossible.

And yes, many observers and reporters repeatedly suggest I routinely used confederates (or "plants," as they are often called) in my audience. Of course, I never have, but I am glad they have made these accusations, and in fact have often jumped on them as an opportunity to generate publicity wherever I appear. There were even times when I would publicize my standing offer:

THE AMAZING KRESKIN WILL PAY ANYONE FIFTY THOUSAND DOLLARS ($50.000.00) WHO PROVES I EMPLOY PAID ASSISTANTS OR CONFEDERATES IN MY PERFORMANCES AND, FURTHERMORE, TO ANYONE WHO CAN PROVE I USE SECRET HIDDEN ELECTRONIC DEVICES TO AID IN THE ACCOMPLISHMENT OF MY THOUGHT- READING DEMONSTRATIONS. THIS CHALLENGE AND ASSURANCE OF INTEGRITY WILL BE VALID THROUGH THE CONTINUANCE OF MY PROFESSIONAL CAREER.

Needless to say, such an offer created exactly the advance buzz I desired. In many instances, this challenge along with appropriate headlines would appear in local newspapers prior to my appearances. As a result, my audiences were often filled with people having but one thought: to try and spot the person or persons who may be aiding Kreskin in achieving his miracles on stage.

Inasmuch as the only assistance I ever utilized came from my own mind, I never worried about having to pay the $50,000.00. In fact, I was to eventually raise the offer to ONE MILLION DOLLARS, where it stands today.

Being able to do the kinds of things I do with the human mind has always set me apart from others who labeled themselves as mind readers. Most of these performers were really just magicians relying on tricks purchased from companies that specialized in supplying conjuring paraphernalia.

Make no mistake: I have no argument with magicians. Like me, they entertain, amuse and, for the most part, amaze. However, their abilities come from purchased apparatus. Mine comes from what is inside my brain.

Frankly, for the most part, I have been very comfortable with the gifts that were given to me. I realize that there is no person in the world that I am aware of who possesses these same abilities. But, I am beginning to grow uneasy about my unique position.

Why?

Because of a vision that came to me while relaxing after a rousing performance in Miami Beach.

Miami Beach has always been a fun town. It is diverse, wonderfully alive and a great place to be able to just bask in its eclectic personality. As usual, the reception I received was amazing. The four curtain calls that resulted were even better. However, what with modern-day cell phones equipped with cameras, my meet-and-greet sessions have grown considerably longer.

Still, these are requests I am always more than happy to accommodate. Admittedly, though, two hours later, I was delighted to finally dive into a multi-course seafood dinner with several friends. After dinner, I retreated to my room for some much-needed rest. I was genuinely tired. A comfortable chair on the balcony of my hotel room was a welcome transition.

I should add that there was a big moon over the ocean, a glass of iced tea sitting at my elbow, and a copy of the *Miami Herald* within arm's reach. This was paradise in the tropics. The only sounds I could hear were the waves breaking over the beach below.

I might note, the moon has always held a fascination for me, an interest I shared with others, particularly Johnny Carson. We both owned telescopes; his was mounted on his roof; mine was hand-held and much less imposing. I cherished it throughout my boyhood years, probably because it always invoked my curiosity and a constant feeling of mysticism of the solar system.

From my vantage point, this was exactly what I needed to rest my body, but it was obviously not enough for my mind, because once again, some unknown force clicked the "Kreskin future" button, and the scene changed abruptly. My next important vision was about to begin.

Somehow, I was cast 10 years into the future. It was the same situation as in other visions: once again, my only function was to be there and observe whatever was to be revealed.

My first objective? To figure out where I was.

It was not easy. All I could determine was that I had been transported to a large, rather plain, sparsely decorated space. Not a hospital. Not a detention room. It looked more like what a hotel room might look like a decade down the line, probably because it contained two neatly made-up queen-sized beds, a night table, a desk and a small sofa.

Directly in my line of vision was what appeared to be a huge television screen (or whatever it might be called 10 years from now). Actually, it occupied the whole wall. It was almost what you might expect in one of today's small multiplex theatres.

On its surface was a news report stating the date, describing some rather cold weather (which, coincidentally, featured a minor blizzard in the mid-west) and someone engaging in considerable small talk about some movie stars who were about to get divorced. (Sorry: in reviewing my notes, I failed to note who they were, although 10 years from now, their names would probably not be recognizable anyhow.)

Other than that, this could have been one of many such programs currently on television — even to the point where the news-commentary seemed to ramble endlessly and switch from topic to topic. What I was watching could have been in the same format utilized today, last month or last year. I found myself intently trying to determine the reason for my being sent into this vision. But not for long, because soon a very startling answer began to emerge.

The newscast switched to a report detailing the government's newest and most successful "mind assist" capabilities.

Mind assist capabilities? What was that all about, I wondered. (NOTE: For years, I have been deeply concerned about the government (ours or anyone else's) possibly gaining control of our thinking. I fear even now that it is happening with individuals and with certain groups throughout the world – both subliminally and by sheer intimidation, covertly and openly.)

From my point of view, such tactics are no different from those relied upon by animal trainers who cruelly turn free-spirited, "born free" jungle beasts into brutalized circus machines by whipping them, stunning them, and motivating them with treats. The result? A complete loss of the free spirit of those animals.

I had seen this happen many times, but there were exceptions. I remember many years ago, while performing at John Ascuaga's Nugget in Sparks, Nevada, observing one particular trainer who had a very popular act with an elephant named Bertha. He somehow had achieved an incredibly loving relationship with the animal, so much so that it enabled him to attempt feats rarely attempted by other trainers. But how was he able to demonstrate this, performance after performance?

As far as I could determine, it was the amazing result of affection and trust between man and beast. In fact, somewhere I have a photo of this magnificent elephant lifting me seven or eight feet in the air using his trunk (and for me to be that fearless, this elephant had to be incredibly gentle and trusting). But sometimes, such affection can backfire.

Such was the case with Siegfried and Roy. For many years, theirs was the "must-see" act on the Las Vegas strip. But one day (and much controversy over this event still exists), one of their tigers mistakenly thought Roy was injured on stage and pulled him away in his teeth as he would an endangered cub. Many thought it was an example of the animal's affection for magician-trainer Roy Horn. There are those who disagree. Regardless, Siegfried and Roy's act was finally over. They had starred on the strip from 1990 to 2003.

But could this "mind assist capability" be a nefarious version of the same thing? Was it now being proposed for humans?

Remember, I was now 10 years into the future. As I began to grasp the significance of what I was now seeing, my attention switched to high alert, which was well justified because someone in a lab coat whom I will simply describe as Dr. Seymour (not his real name, but as far as I was concerned, it could have been Dr. Svengali) was now describing what this "mind assist capability" was all about.

It is important that I note that Dr. Seymour came across almost like one of those loveable "friendly uncle" types, the kind you would see on a Saturday morning kids' show. Only this uncle identified himself as a psychiatrist, scientist, and co-developer of MA-1, short for "Mind Assist-1." Even the name was troubling.

From the way he talked, I assumed the viewing public had been prepped for what he was now saying and that this was possibly the result of advance publicity, newspaper articles, and greatly hyped speculation.

Still, *I* had no idea what was to come. That made me even more anxious to hear his remarks. However, it did not take long for his intent to become frighteningly clear. What this carefully chosen, likeable, authoritative individual was pitching was terrifying.

My worst fears seemed as though they would soon turn to possible reality. It seems Dr. Seymour was talking about an incredible new use for what we currently refer to as nano chips (keep in mind, I was eavesdropping 10 years into the future). It seemed these tiny chips had advanced significantly enough in their development to enable MA-1 to be talked of as a possible solution to all future ignorance in the entire world, as Dr. Seymour put it, "a marvelous gift to children yet to be born."

I still did not know how they would be utilized. But not to worry – Dr. Seymour soon supplied the answer.

He explained that these nanochips were electrical circuits the size of a nanometer (which he was now referring to as a microgen). But here was the part that I was bracing for: he described how science would now be able to implant them at the base of a newborn baby's skull.

Once these chips were in position, no child would ever fail to comprehend what they were being taught, regardless of whether it was on an elementary, high school or college level, or even beyond.

Consequently, brilliance would be commonplace and no one would be smarter than anyone else. Furthermore, any and all communicated information would be permanent and incapable of being forgotten, erased or affected by any age or medically related memory loss.

Sounds like a real positive step forward, right? Wrong.

Here is the most troubling factor of what MA-1 would introduce into our society: these chips implanted in infants could be controlled, communicated with, and even made to cause all kinds of mental pain.

Once this became possible, these children would be vulnerable to outside direct commands, additional instructions, non-contested political philosophy, and even torture. The result? The very real possibility of our becoming a society of drones, future adults with minds dependent on outside intrusion anytime, anyplace, and anywhere.

I kept watching, aghast at what was being revealed on the screen in front of me. I kept thinking, "Could this ever really occur?"

In 10 years, by 2023, children coming into this world would be subject to a form of mind control called MIND ASSIST-1?! As if I was not already shocked at what this vision was revealing, it was what came next that startled and troubled me even more.

It seems already in a design stage was MA-2, which would allow key governmental control centers to actually read minds. Such mind penetration, according to Dr. Seymour, would be limited only to individuals deemed potential enemies to our country.

Of course, all of this was being spoken of as if it was not only a significant step forward in generating a higher level of achievement, but also in creating greater assurance for the world's security.

I remember a little man with a moustache preaching similar thoughts. I realize a whole generation of future geniuses might sound appealing to some. The truth is, such a concept is hateful from every aspect. In reality, it is the much-feared intrusion of Orwell's Big Brother into every facet of our lives.

Actually, it is considerably more than that. If what I saw comes to pass—and by now, you can hear that the chorus of this book is that I hope that it never does—everything we envisioned, fought for, and died for when we first became a nation would be permanently devastated by rampant technology in the hands of irresponsible leaders.

It was at this point that my vision came to an abrupt end. It was so real, I had no idea as to how long I had experienced this unsettling look into the future. I swear I was not asleep. This was another genuine vision that left me noticeably shaken and, in fact, angry. But why to such a greater degree this time than after other such vision experiences?

Because the human mind is the last refuge for free thought, creative expression, and ideas that can heal, build, and maintain peace. Once its control is wrested from us, we become a nation of mental clones, marching to a central drumbeat.

Yes, Hitler was able to bring this about by his dramatic skills as an orator and manipulator of massive misdirected hysteria. Back at the height of his power, in a book written by Professor of Psychology Dr. George H. Estabrooks titled *Hypnotism*, he referred to Adolph Hitler as the most powerful hypnotist he had ever publically heard speak.

Even today, nearly 60 years after Hitler's death, world scholars still ponder how this personification of unabashed evil could command rapt attention and transfix mass minds just by the power of his words, his body language, and his absolute conviction that his mission was directed by a higher power that could never fail.

Now we face the prospect of a new form of reckless mind control, achieved by runaway technology that seemingly has no bounds. Our problem is that we may not be able to control into whose hands it may fall.

Again, I can only hope and pray that this is another one of my visions that will not come to pass.

The rapid direction of technology has me greatly concerned. My greatest fear is that the last vestige of privacy left to man will be eliminated. This would create a crisis far more powerful than a nuclear attack. Not only would it be the elimination of man's private thoughts, but both the elimination of his ability to create independently and his ability to defend against the loss of personal freedoms and necessary rights.

In effect, a chaotic happening that would hammer a spike into the heart of positive human evolution and independent genius.

Here again, there has to be a purpose for this deeply troubling vision. Perhaps it is for me to write about it, talk about it, and in any and all other ways draw attention to its troubling consequences.

PICK A CARD, ANY CARD

A number of weeks later, I flew into Philadelphia for an afternoon lecture before a local organization of active business leaders.

Even in a situation such as this one, I like to establish my "credentials" early. The truth is, even though this was primarily a non-demonstration appearance, I almost never let such occasions pass without performing at least one "effect" to cause my audience to wonder how a seemingly mere mortal can accomplish what can only accurately be described as a mind miracle. I also realize that when people hear the name Kreskin they think of the "M" word: "magician."

I detest being categorized as such, which is another reason why I like to do something special early on that will prevent me from later being referred to as a magician. Trust me, with the word "Amazing" before my name, this is often necessary. Still, in most instances it takes no more than a few minutes to extrude the same "oohs" and "ahhs" one might expect to hear during one of those celebrity-billed illusion magic shows, only more so.

As it turned out, my lecture went over very well. There was a dinner that followed where I was seated next to several elected Pennsylvania legislators. One of them mentioned he had seen me perform on stage in Atlantic City and wondered if I was likely to appear in one of their state's own spectacular new casinos.

(NOTE: My answer, of course, was yes. I always welcome new venues. And over the years, I have enjoyed observing the differences in audiences. Furthermore, it was no secret some of the world's biggest casino corporations were leading the charge to plant alluring palaces in strategic locations in the Keystone state.)

But one thing remained constant: I always had a soft spot for Atlantic City. After all, I am a native of New Jersey and had watched AC's transition from a popular honeymoon and family destination to the second-largest gambling Mecca in the U.S. (a position it no longer holds).

As it turned out, the legislator's reference to Atlantic City was timely, because I had a meeting scheduled there the next day. Although I have a very able staff to arrange my schedule, I wanted to handle this next booking myself; it was with an old friend and one of the town's top casino entertainment directors, and I welcomed the chance to see him again.

It was an approximately 50-mile trip from Philadelphia to AC on the Atlantic City Expressway. I had made this drive many times, but rarely had the traffic been so light. Noticeable, too, was a subdued tone radiating from the billboards along the way. Over the years, they had shouted out the praises of their particular casino destinations, the fantastic jackpots, the bonus points for play, the superstars appearing in their showrooms, the restaurant and buffet bargains, and so on. Now there seemed to be a subdued sense of enthusiasm.

The hour's trip went fast, and my meeting immediately switched from my friend's office to one of the town's high roller restaurants: Harrah's Steakhouse, a place that I particularly enjoyed.

But there was a method to his madness; after ordering a cocktail for himself and some ice water for me, he tossed a sealed deck of playing cards on the restaurant table and waved to an acquaintance across the room.

He quickly introduced us, even though I also had known this chap for years. This person was a top casino executive who just "happened" to be sitting close by. I was beginning to suspect this was a setup, particularly after I recalled that my host always requested I perform this one specific "mind miracle" using cards; my hunch was that he probably wanted an additional pair of eyes to determine how I did what I did.

I am not thrilled when I am asked to demonstrate my skills out of the blue, but I figured it was easier to comply than to say no. What's more, I realized he was going to pay the check, which for a dinner in this eating establishment was not cheap. Therefore, I requested each of them to thoroughly shuffle the deck.

I should point out that I wanted this to be quick but impressive. The thought of one of this restaurant's renowned meals was fanning my hunger.

I asked my friend to think of any card he saw as I riffled the deck in front of him. In doing so, I made a point to emphasize that I had not requested him to remove the card or disclose it to anyone else. Just think of it.

Next, I shuffled the deck and removed three cards from the bottom and had him confirm that none of these choices was the card he had thought of. Then, with the cards turned downward and sitting on the table away from my hands or control, I told him to touch any one of them, which he did readily. In fact, I told him to place his hand firmly on the down card he touched, so as to further assure that I could not get to it even if I wanted to.

Finally, I re-described the steps to the two of them: 1) They both had thoroughly shuffled the deck; 2) My friend had freely thought of any card when I riffled the deck in front of him without requesting him to remove the card, only to continue thinking of it; 3) I then shuffled the cards once more and removed the bottom three cards from the deck and showed them to him; and 4) He affirmed that none of these cards was the one he thought of.

I was now ready to once again demonstrate the power of the human mind. But first, I reminded him that the card he had thought of had not been among any of the three I placed in front of him and therefore could not possibly be hidden among any of the three.

Moreover, I emphasized that his hand was still firmly pressed against one that he randomly chose and that it would be an absolute miracle if it turned out to actually be the card he thought of.

He agreed without hesitation.

By now, I was talking a little louder and a number of people from neighboring tables had gathered around. Of course, that being the case, my stage persona kicked in. It was certainly evident when, with grand aplomb, I asked him to name the card he thought of.

"The three of diamonds," he replied, absolutely confident that the card he was still protecting was anything but that card. After all, he had seen the ones that had been turned face down in front of him. None of them was that card.

I then requested him to turn over the card beneath his palm.

When he lifted his hand, he revealed the three of diamonds. His mouth fell open. Applause broke out in the immediate area. Once again, he was a participant in the *impossible*. Happily, my success was rewarded with a generous-sized filet mignon.

It was several hours later when I had returned to my hotel room. I had been gifted with a large suite usually reserved for VIPs and high rollers. The bed was soft, and I welcomed the prospects of sinking into it and grabbing some much-needed sleep. However, I wanted first to complete a late jog, my daily custom.

It took mere minutes to put on my running clothes and step out onto possibly the world's most famous boardwalk. It was now early evening. The weather was mild, and the lights of Atlantic City's casinos were now turning on. As usual, they were spectacular to behold.

I decided to run approximately one mile, from the Tropicana to the Taj Mahal. Once again, I was a little surprised by the lack of people traffic. Usually, the boardwalk was packed at this hour, but still, I did not give it much thought. That was to come later, in another profound vision.

VISION NO. 9

The Gambling Begins, and the Magic of the Original Atlantic City is Lost Forever

———————◦~◦~◦———————

It's funny how you stash memories of your childhood. Many of mine involve my early trips to Atlantic City with my parents; there was so much to see, smell, and taste. In that regard, the food in Atlantic City was among the best on America's East Coast. Particular favorites of my family were destinations such as Tony's Bar & Grill, Captain Starn's, and Hackney's Seafood Restaurant. There were others, but these stand out.

I also have vivid memories of the Miss America Pageant, as Bert Parks sang out, "There she is, Miss America." It was always an important television event and one our nation waited to see year after year.

Thinking back, the earliest pageant I remember was as a pre-teenager, when in 1945 a stunning Bess Myerson (a former Miss New York) won the crown. She was beautiful and went on to a career in television and eventually in politics. Miss America winners and even the finalists often moved on to success in other fields.

The Atlantic City pageants actually contributed to busy times and opportunities for me as a last minute fill-in or substitute for gigs in nearby small clubs that later grew into more important appearances, all the while allowing me to perfect my skills. Nevertheless, I always found time to behold this fabulous town in total awe.

There were the crowds on Steel Pier, the original Fralinger's Salt Water Taffy being twisted and packaged fresh right in front of strollers' eyes, Madame Tussaud's Wax Museum, and the famed Mr. Peanut, who headquartered at a Planters retail store at the north end of the boardwalk.

Other attractions included the many bathhouses and numerous auction venues that pulled in bargain hunters and curiosity seekers. All of these places are now gone forever, sacrificed to the gambling frenzy that took hold of the town in 1978 when an enabling referendum paved the way for the opening of Resorts International.

I remember its introduction well because one of its future supporters, Merv Griffin, was someone I admired greatly. In fact, I made no fewer than 101 appearances on his TV show. We bonded well, and I will always treasure the special interest he demonstrated in my abilities. It delighted me how he reacted to my minor miracles much like the people who purchased expensive front-row seats to my performances. Very often, his facial expressions were of total amazement, and this was a man who daily met with and saw the premier singers and actors of the time.

Resorts International opened to considerable fanfare and bustling crowds. People could not wait to get in and to do so, they had to be properly attired with a jacket and tie. If they wanted to stay or vacation, arrangements had to be made well in advance. However, by the time the 1980s arrived, the excitement had dimmed considerably. Resorts was no longer the only kid on the block. In fact, the history-making casino now needed substantial updating.

To make matters worse, brand new gambling palaces sprung up all along the boardwalk—and no longer was a dress code required anywhere. Soon, Resorts' profits turned to losses, and in 1988 a battle ensued between entertainer Merv Griffin and realty tycoon Donald Trump. After two months of give-and-take, Griffin obtained control of Resorts along with another casino in the Bahamas, and Trump acquired the rights to the Taj Mahal which had been part of Resorts International holdings.

Sadly, the much-admired Merv Griffin is no longer with us, but Trump's name still looms large over the Taj, even though he actually owns little or no part of what was once considered AC's most glamorous resort.

As these somewhat ancient thoughts ran through my mind, I hardly noticed that nightfall had subtly descended on the many edifices of this legendary resort community.

With the coming of evening, I no longer felt in a hurry to get back. I decided that instead of jogging southward on the boardwalk, I would walk on the sand alongside the water. In that way, I could enjoy the dual pleasure of having on one side of me the glittering expanse of the Atlantic Ocean, and on the other, a pastiche of flashing colors projecting from the lights of the various casinos.

The night had become marvelously clear. As I stared at the boardwalk, I could see the silhouettes of not only players parading through various casino doors, but also bicycle riders, late joggers like myself, and occasional couples strolling hand in hand. It made me think how quickly we forget that Atlantic City was once one of America's most popular honeymoon destinations.

As I continued walking, I just wanted to "milk" all of the pleasure of what I was observing. It was not too often that I could experience this kind of soul food for the mind. However, I was becoming a little tired.

Almost as if fate chose my next resting place, I came upon a somewhat antiquated seagoing rescue boat bearing the words ATLANTIC CITY. It was lying upside down on the sand, obviously placed there for use as a photo stop. From my point of view, it was the perfect place for me to sit on its stern and look out at the sea. Little did I realize I was about to be whisked a long way from this idyllic spot.

I had been facing the water, watching the distant lights of fishing boats a few miles off shore on the horizon. Somehow, for some reason, I felt compelled to turn around and once again face the boardwalk. However, what now greeted my eyes was startling.

Gone were the lights. Gone were most of the people. Gone was the aura of excitement. It was almost as if someone had turned off the switch on Atlantic City. Stunned by this incredible transition, I found myself walking in the sand, heading for steps that would take me up on the boardwalk.

Once there, I had a better view of what now appeared in front of me. Incredibly, the very first casino I saw had plywood nailed to all three of its front doors. As I continued walking, another once-proud resort also had plywood blocking its entrance. Further down the boardwalk I could see some occasional lights of fast food places and even a few people. Of course, as in previous visions, I could not interact with any of them. What I saw next surprised me even more.

High above me, on what appeared to be the 15th floor of one of the town's proudest gambling meccas, was a banner proclaiming condos for sale, from $85,000 to $150,000 each. It struck me that the very least these offerings should be going for was a figure five times as much.

By now, I was desperately trying to determine where I was in time. What year had my vision transported me to? As I continued walking, I eventually saw one of those honor system boxes that contained newspapers. It was obvious it had not been opened for a long while. Its glass surface was covered with encrusted dust. Yet it still contained newspapers. I quickly reached inside to pull one of them out. The date I saw was 2018, which probably meant this incredible transformation of Atlantic City had occurred far earlier.

It is interesting that when I looked at the headline of the paper, it contained pretty much the same nonsense going in our current time. With all of this happening, I felt a need to walk over to the railing separating the boardwalk from the sea. However, when I grasped it, it immediately separated me from my trip into the future.

All of a sudden, I was back to the here and now. People were walking past me, casino lights were glowing brightly, gamblers were moving to and from their destinations. Then I realized, I had been transferred ahead to an Atlantic City that soon may be —unless something is done to prevent my vision from turning to reality.

As I indicated earlier in this book, I have no idea why I was swept into these visions. Certainly, they had been coming at all hours, under all kinds of circumstances: sometimes while I was in a near dream state, other times while I felt I was experiencing some kind of attack, and even during times such as this, while I was merely resting comfortably watching the sea.

However, this vision disturbed me particularly, because of the likelihood that it would actually come true. As indicated previously, I have a fond attachment to Atlantic City and would sincerely regret seeing it morph into hard to sell high-rise towers left to the mercies of nature and economic circumstance.

Still, circumstances now affecting this town may be very slowly sounding its death knell. Even as I stood on the boardwalk after my vision, it was plain that this was no longer the Atlantic City of old. Yes, there were still plenty of people on the boardwalk, but they were not the throngs that used to be shoulder-to-shoulder on this famous New Jersey site. Furthermore, crowds inside the casinos were substantially smaller, and these days, anyone wanting a room on the spur of the moment can readily find any accommodations they desire.

But what are the other circumstances threatening Atlantic City?

For starters, to the east are numerous casinos spread across the state of Pennsylvania, thereby greatly reducing the number of players coming from Philadelphia and other parts of that state. To the south are the slot destinations in Maryland. To the north is the most hurtful threat of all: casino gambling at New York's Aqueduct and Empire racetracks, which offer slot players a much closer and less time-consuming option to the three-to-four-hour trip to Atlantic City.

There are other factors, as well. Atlantic City's rules for popular table games benefit the house much more than in other nearby destinations. Players simply do not have the favorable options offered in venues in competing states. Furthermore, there are stories about how their slots are near impossible to hit and possibly the icing on the cake is the hefty parking fees they impose.

Taking all of this into account, it is easy to reason that the writing is on the wall for this once-treasured seaside resort. The problem is, it probably is too late to erase.

My visions were to continue. However, my next one was more uplifting.

THE NEW WORLD

For most of my life, I have maintained the utmost faith in our country, its goals and its leaders—in its brightest days and in its darkest.

As a youngster, I watched with pride its emergence from World War II, Eisenhower became President, followed by a charismatic Kennedy; I watched its passage of bills to ensure the education and well-being of its veterans, its continued growth as an economic power, its successful landing of a man on the moon, and much much more. This was America at its best, an America adhering to its destiny.

Something happened.

Suddenly, ominous seeds of change began to darken our horizons. Stories were appearing about our being involved in something called a Cold War. The USSR was accused of having missile silos based in Cuba, and boats were en route loaded with atomic warheads; here at home, events had also begun to turn ugly.

Innocent men and women were being blacklisted from their professions because of so-called, often-unproven Communist affiliations. Children were being prevented from entering certain schools because of the color of their skin. Civil rights workers were being murdered by cowards wearing hoods.

In the midst of all of this, the unthinkable happened: two of the greatest leaders of our time, John F. Kennedy and Martin Luther King Jr., were assassinated.

The years that followed continued the seemingly downward spiral of our hopes, our dreams, and our own perceptions of what we stood for. There was the debacle in Vietnam, Watergate, Clinton's involvement with an intern that caused his impeachment, the government's mis-assessment of the aftermath of the Iraq war, the collapse of the U.S. housing market, and the subsequent recession. Sadly, these negative events continued year after year, right up to this moment.

Even as you read this, political parties are at each other's throats. The media has been divided into various camps. Unemployment continues. And there seems to be no one specific person in either party who can truly articulate a unifying direction.

Up until recently, I foresaw very little chance of America returning to its former position as the most respected nation in the world. Who would lead us? Who might unite us? Who might raise the voice of reason?

Certainly, I did not perceive the resurrection of our original founding fathers. Nothing like that could ever happen again. Or could it?

VISION NO. 10

A New Leader Emerges

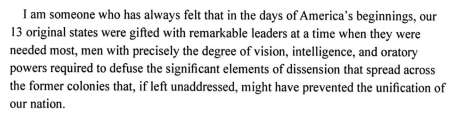

I am someone who has always felt that in the days of America's beginnings, our 13 original states were gifted with remarkable leaders at a time when they were needed most, men with precisely the degree of vision, intelligence, and oratory powers required to defuse the significant elements of dissension that spread across the former colonies that, if left unaddressed, might have prevented the unification of our nation.

Was the presence of these men at this particular time (and each having a voice that commanded attention and respect) some strange accident?

Was their coming together in Philadelphia that hot summer of 1776 the result of: 1. Divine intervention? 2. A coincidental convergence of widely divergent opinion? 3. A congregation of brilliance unlike anything seen before or since?

I tend to go with "divine intervention."

Here is why:

One needs only to consider who these people were: Benjamin Franklin, Thomas Jefferson, Samuel Adams, Alexander Hamilton, John Jay, James Madison, George Washington, and others of near greatness. Imagine all of them drawn by circumstance to a steamy room in Philadelphia to draft a Constitution that would stand as the backbone of America's strength for approximately 250 years.

Also consider, each was a giant in his own right. And each, if living in a different time in our history, probably would have been considered a significant figure based merely on his own achievements.

But here they were, brought together for a task that could not have been achieved by any lesser group; certainly not even by any hand-picked super-achievers of the 21st century.

This is why I lean toward the divine option. I can only conclude that the role of the collective greatness of our forefathers was to specifically create a nation like no other.

But did they totally succeed, and is this country of ours still on course to fulfill its intended mission? Certainly, our record since the passage of our Constitution has not been without its share of national disgrace and blemishes.

For starters, there was the unfair treatment of our country's Native Americans. This is a particularly prominent scar on our historical record.

It continued with the authorization of raids slaughtering thousands of Indians by Andrew Jackson (in so-called retaliation for killings of Americans during the early border wars).

Next came the nullification of treaties that prevented the government from forcing Native Americans from their reservations, which many observers believed was to accommodate the railroads and large companies prospecting for gold.

But our mistakes did not stop there.

Later, there was the internment of thousands of innocent Japanese citizens at the outbreak of World War II and, most decidedly, the intolerance that led to the assassinations of the Kennedy brothers, Martin Luther King Jr. and Malcolm X.

It is hard to say why all these thoughts were filling my mind before my next vision occurred. Possibly because I had been requested to perform at a party for a major leader in government affairs. He was what most insiders would call a "mover and shaker" in Washington, one of a select few who is appointed to key committees, who is considered as a possible candidate for an upcoming election (regardless of party), and even who might be chosen as a keynote speaker for the upcoming conventions.

(NOTE: I had long ago come to realize that both parties were run by the same puppet master. More about this in my next book.)

Actually, this was the second time this very special individual had requested my services at one of his functions. I felt flattered and somewhat surprised that I was still on his short list of preferred entertainers. Why?

Because even though I try to avoid politics when I am interviewed, on occasion I do let my dissatisfaction with the current direction of our country slip out. Consequently, I was certain my comments had probably drifted back to the influential top guys who run this nation — my host being one of them.

But here I was.

Furthermore, I was told the President might actually drop by. I kept thinking I would love a photo-op with the Commander-in-Chief. Needless to say, as the time approached for me to begin my presentation, I kept watching the door, hoping to see President Obama come walking through. In fact, I actually dragged my feet somewhat in getting started with my portion of the evening's entertainment.

To my utter disappointment, he never appeared. I kept thinking what an experience it might have been, perhaps talking to the world's most powerful leader. As it turned out, I had to settle for some chit-chatting with members of the House and the Senate, a number of lobbyists, and a few of their wives.

I might mention that if I had tuned in to some of what was really occupying the minds of these very powerful people, I probably would have found myself both fascinated and frightened. Fortunately, I resisted temptation for any intrusion into private areas of their subconscious.

Nevertheless, I wondered what some of these high-level guests would have thought of the possibility of Kreskin actually being able to read their minds. I am sure the Secret Service, knowing I would be in attendance, probably had given this potential mental intrusion some consideration.

The entertainment portion of the party had begun. There were several singers, a rock band and The Amazing Kreskin. I performed for approximately 45 well-received minutes. This was followed by numerous questions as I made my way back into the crowd. Luckily, it ended with the announcement that dinner was being served.

It turned out to be a wonderful feast; there was a generous assortment of entrees, and naturally, I chose from the seafood selections: my choices consisted of a hearty shrimp cocktail, New England clam chowder, and wild salmon accompanied by vegetables and breads, followed by a wide choice of pastries, pies and ice cream. But the part of the dinner I savored most was a toast by my host, saluting my performance.

Here I was, The Amazing Kreskin, being celebrated by some of the most renowned of our country's leaders.

When I was a kid in grammar school I remember being warned that my marks had better improve or I'd never make it in the real world. At that particular moment, I would have loved to have a few of my old teachers see me now.

When the dinner was over, I was enjoying a patriotic high; all around me were walls bedecked with portraits of many of our country's most famous figures. Standing in front of them, I could see small clusters of the rich, the famous and the powerful, all caught up in matters of national and international importance.

I do not know how many times I heard the word "budget" bandied about or discussions regarding various bills coming up for a vote. But deep down, I loved this milieu. The hours flew by and the festivities would soon wound down.

But the evening was not quite over for me, because my host had arranged for a limousine to take me to and from the party. I had never felt more important. I had never felt more valued. This was a night to be remembered. However, I soon came to realize there were other reasons this would become an evening I would not soon forget.

Back at my hotel, my mind continued to focus on the people I had met. Yet, when matching them up to the huge problems confronting our country, I was somewhat troubled. Could any of the powerful individuals I met that night, or for that matter, anyone else reverse the damage caused by the distrust, poor communications, and inexperience that currently permeates the high-level corridors of Washington? I thought not.

Unfortunately, these ills have put a stranglehold on our nation's confidence, elevated our insecurity, and tarnished the world's perception of America as the world's superpower.

These were the thoughts that filled my mind upon my return to my hotel room. In fact, they were sufficient to interfere with any likelihood of sleep. Consequently, I found myself doing mundane things to pass the time: working on a crossword puzzle, evaluating my next day's schedule, and finally, dialing room service for a wake-up call even though I was convinced I would probably remain awake for the rest of the night.

One of the advantages of my hotel was that it provided a great view of our Nation's capital; plainly visible were many of our most well-known buildings and monuments. This was the kind of vantage point networks always desired as the background for correspondents reporting from Washington.

That is probably why I found myself standing up, peering through the drapes. Washington at night is a startling sight. I put it right up there with New York City and Las Vegas; each is spectacular in its own right, and each is unforgettable. As I looked out at the darkness, I could see both the Capitol dome and the Washington Monument.

Their artificial illumination was augmented by the glow of a full moon. Around them was a dazzling array of twinkling lights coming from a wide assortment of sources. Some were from lines of cars still backed up in traffic, others from government offices open 24 hours, still more from jet planes coming and going. I could not help thinking that each light probably had a story to tell.

I pulled the drapes together and settled back in a large leather chair. Still not really tired, I let my head rest against its back.

And then it happened again, as suddenly and as incredibly as usual.

I was now in a completely different place. It was outdoors and immediately identifiable as one of the world's most visited sites.

(NOTE: At this point, I must continue to urge you to maintain your trust in what I am revealing. Remember, like all my other visions, there is a profound reason why I have been chosen to experience what is made known to me.)

The spot where I now found myself was in front of the Lincoln Memorial. I was all alone.

I looked up at the statue of The Great Emancipator, who, in his sculpted magnificence, made me feel truly insignificant. I heard a strong, resonant, and impressive voice.

My first reaction was to rapidly walk around the monument, thinking there was someone present who was possibly hiding for some unknown reason. I also looked for hidden amplifiers that might be responsible for the rich and impressive sound of the voice I heard. In both instances, I found nothing. Keep in mind, although I realized there was no rational reason for my even being there, I considered myself wide awake and in perfect control of my mental faculties.

As the voice continued to speak, I was careful to take mental note of what I heard resounding throughout the Memorial rotunda.

What I am describing here is from my written notes. It is not word for word, but it closely represents the message given to me.

Specifically, I was told that in the months ahead, there would be someone whose visibility would increase significantly. Although this person would not run as a candidate for the office of President in 2016, he would in 2020. This individual – through charisma, intelligence, ability to cut through political barriers and to talk to ALL people, would capture the imagination, trust and respect of not only Americans, but of people in countries throughout the world.

But as is the case with anyone whose appeal seems to resonate with the majority of his listeners, he would be attacked viciously. Nevertheless, the allure and attraction of this candidate will enable him to overcome these barriers and capture the office of President of the United States by a landslide.

I was further told that this individual would greatly unite this country and eventually end many of its problems.

The bottom line seems to be that we need only wait: The much-needed help is in the wings, raring to go and ready to make his voice heard.

There were some additional clues that came through, but I am not sure whether this strange voice wanted me to reveal my speculations as to who this person might be. I am afraid that if I were to specify a name now, it would cause problems down the line.

Incidentally, in case you are wondering whether the voice I heard was that of Abraham Lincoln, I am fairly sure it was not. From everything I have read, (and I have conducted considerable research since this experience, regarding what he actually sounded like) Lincoln's voice was much higher than the one speaking to me that night.

I should also add that this encounter ended as suddenly as it began. The transition to my room was immediate. In the blink of an eye, I was back in the chair, wide awake and positively amazed at what had just transpired.

FURTHER CLARIFICATION REGARDING MY VISIONS

———— ⟐ ————

First off, I wish to emphasize that I am in perfect health; spectacular, I might add, considering my constant traveling, the many hours spent in the air, and the many questionable restaurants I am forced to eat in.

Nevertheless (as mentioned earlier in this book), these visions come to me in many strange ways. Sometimes in a manner similar to the onset of a stroke or just a feeling of sickness. Other times while I am just resting but still wide awake. And still others are like an instantaneous transition to wherever and whenever.

Throughout my life, I have had visions, but few as significant as the ones I am describing here. These have come in close succession in the last five years—and particularly in the last two.

What's more, I have never felt about them as I do now. This is the reason why I am on a personal mission to report them to you, the reader, in order to publicize them wherever and however possible to the world. In that way, those visions that foretell of negative happenings might in some unforeseen manner be lessened, turned around to produce a positive outcome or be totally prevented.

Admittedly, I believe in miracles.

I also want to clarify the difference between these visions and when I make predictions. Over the years, I have made many predictions covering a wide range of subjects. Predictions are my personal instinctive "perceptions" of things to come. They are not visions. To be sure, they may sometimes be affected by my own subconscious processing of current events which, when blended with unexplainable insight into a potential subject of general concern, can affect a prediction. As such, they may be less accurate than I would hope for. Still, too many of them have come true for me to not give them appropriate attention.

They are far different from my visions, which are happenings somewhere in the future that I have been given the privilege of observing, and I am an observer only.

VISION No. 11

The Dead Are Resurrected

I have long been fascinated with any kind of science fiction that deals with bringing the dead back to life. Accordingly, I believe that before this century is over (and not too many years from now, if my vision comes true), the ability to restore life will definitely be achieved. In fact, so much so that resurrection of people who have been declared clinically dead will become commonplace.

I am not talking about making Hollywood's "Frankenstein" perception of that happen. The movie makers achieved it by depicting the theft of a freshly executed corpse, giving it a new brain, attaching some electric connections to protrusions in its neck, and then hoisting it up to the ceiling where it could be repeatedly jolted by "life-giving" lightning. This hardly will be the way it will come to pass.

Given that this is just dramatized claptrap, could such a miracle really happen? Actually, it already has!

True! At a well-respected Pennsylvania hospital, researchers have experimented with a technique that is already bringing the dead back to life.

How? By initiation of an experimental treatment using chilled saline that is injected directly into the body of the deceased patient. The body temperature, normally 98 degrees, is brought down to just 92 degrees. Doctors keep it there for about 24 hours. This is called intentional hypothermia.

According to one of the doctors who helped develop the process, "it decreases cellular injury to the body." With less injury to the cells, doctors are now able to do what was once considered impossible: bring the dead back to life.

In fact, they recently used the technique to revive a 61-year-old man who collapsed in front of his home. After he fell, his heart stopped beating. According to his wife, he was definitely dead. "It was the most frightening thing I ever saw in my life," she said. "I knew my husband was gone. He was gone forever."

Fortunately, he was taken to the Pennsylvania hospital where this technique had been developed. Upon arrival, doctors quickly initiated their new methodology to bring him back. The man is now alive and fully functioning.

Doctors at the hospital are continuing to improve their life-saving protocol, by developing a new "slushy" kind of saline that is full of small ice particles. This will enable the doctors to inject it directly into the bloodstream to more rapidly reduce body temperature. They are hopeful it will eventually become a critical standard of care in bringing dead patients back to life. But, that is just one hospital and one methodology under study.

Halfway around the world, doctors at an Australian hospital are also resurrecting the clinically dead. They have developed two methods that have already performed life- restoring miracles, achieved with three patients who were officially declared dead for periods of 40 to 60 minutes.

One procedure utilizes a machine called the AutoPulse, a portable CPR device that performs constant chest compressions that essentially keep the heart of a dead person beating. The other is a technique called Extracorporeal Membrane Oxygenation (ECMO), which for all practical purposes simulates the action of a lung outside the body that keeps oxygen and blood flowing to the patient's brain and vital organs.

ECMO has been used in the past for lung transplant recipients as well as for extremely ill newborns, but now the combination of ECMO and the Auto Pulse has proved remarkable in restoring life to the clinically deceased.

I have described these two particular methods of life restoration because they are dependent on machines and techniques that may not necessarily be new, but when used together, can produce miraculous results. Yet, as admirable as they are, and as important as they are, they will someday be looked upon as highly primitive "patch and paste" approaches to reviving the dead.

There are other imaginative, cutting-edge approaches being developed throughout the world achieving similar results.

I have little doubt that someday in the future all such methods will be like comparing the Wright Brothers' first flying machine with the supersonic jets now so commonplace.

The question remains: will there be a singular brilliant method that will bypass everything achieved by previous researchers?

If the vision that came to me just about two months ago comes to pass: yes.

Before I go any further, I want to emphasize that when the vision I am about to describe occurred, it came at a time when there was no reason why restoring the dead should have even found a niche in my subconscious. Still, in determining what could have been its genesis, the answer might have come from one of those zombie movies I watched earlier one night in my hotel room overlooking a cemetery in the outskirts of Baton Rouge, Louisiana. Consequently, it is easy to conclude that the setting was appropriate.

To be clear, I am usually much more discriminating in choosing what I expose my mind to on television. But when choices are limited, I figure that at the very least, a zombie movie might be good for a few laughs.

Please also understand, my exposure to television is dictated by my wild schedule. On any given day, I might be catching some much-needed shuteye while zooming across America at 30,000 feet, or I might be meeting with a producer. Or I might actually be appearing on some distant stage in front of a thousand people.

Therefore, my ability to stay loyal to any specific network or series is limited. I definitely live in the world of "catch as catch can" TV, which why I occasionally watch something as dreadful as a zombie movie.

But rather than dwell on why it may have happened, allow me to describe the vision as it drew me into a place far removed from this gloomy room overlooking a cemetery.

Once again, my transition to this vision caught me completely by surprise.

I had gotten up from the bed in which I was sitting to draw the drapes of the room's window closed, to block the dreary view below. But when I turned to once again seat myself on the bed, I found that I was now in an entirely different place. Somehow, some way, I was amidst an audience filled with what appeared to be hundreds of media news people.

In front of them was a stage occupied by four men and three women. Two of them were wearing what appeared to be hospital scrubs. The others were in normal business attire. Alongside the group was a huge screen.

One of the group spoke into a microphone and called for everyone's attention. When the room became silent, he introduced himself and prefaced his remarks by saying he was about to confirm results the world had been waiting to hear for centuries...

THE DEAD CAN LIVE AGAIN

Of course I was startled by such a statement; I even looked around to see if there was any laughter from the audience. There was none. Good thing, for I was soon to witness incredible proof that not only can such a miracle be made to happen, but also that those who brought back were usually in better health than during the five years prior to their passing.

You have to understand what was going through my mind. Here I was, The Amazing Kreskin, about to see actual proof that the dead could be resurrected. One of the key goals of mankind was about to be demonstrated before my very eyes.

The doctor began with a long speech tracing humanity's journey from its very beginnings to where we were on this fateful day. The doctor, using a laptop computer, went on to narrate a series of graphics that began flashing on a large screen in front of us.

As he went from visual to visual, he discussed the relevance of everything depicted. This included various organs, nerves, arteries, the brain, the heart, muscles and the many internal systems that are vital to life.

Unlike his opening comments, which were overly long and purposely technical, this presentation now seemed easier to follow, though still not easy enough for me to keep up with the many flowcharts, graphic illustrations, and medical terms flying by. As a result, I soon found myself somewhat mystified and slightly confused.

Others in the audience—not so. I noticed they seemed to be nodding as if they understood everything. I had to assume these people were not just ordinary media people, but probably other physicians and medical writers representing a wide range of news media.

It must have been 15 minutes into the session when the doctor who had initiated the presentation sat down and was replaced by a second doctor who introduced himself and signaled for maximum attention.

(NOTE: Each doctor was introduced by name, but I am purposefully not including them in this book, primarily because what I was witnessing was happening in the future. Such disclosures at this time would raise heightened expectations of their current performance and possibly affect their medical careers.)

It was now evident that as each of the speakers made their presentation, a heightened mood of expectation was building. And it was justified.

As if the suspense was too much to bear any longer, or perhaps on cue, the speaker once again called for everyone's attention. I sensed that I might now be treated to the "main event," actual proof that the dead could be revived. It was worth the wait.

He soon informed us that what we were about to see was an actual video of a deceased individual being brought back to life.

My excitement grew stronger.

He went on to describe the individual in this video as having died approximately four days earlier, but the preliminary procedures prepping him for revival were recorded six hours prior to this presentation.

With that pronouncement, the screen darkened, and we were now viewing what appeared to be an operating room, probably in the same hospital where we congregated. Somehow, I felt I was watching the scene in the movie *King Kong,* where the curtains roll back and the shackled great beast is introduced to a crowded nightclub audience.

But what I was seeing was hardly a wild beast tugging on his restraints: this was a real person, who we were told was an adult male of 47, severely injured in an auto accident and pronounced dead four days earlier. As far as could be determined from what we were viewing on the TV screen, there was no reason not to believe he was physically dead.

However, what followed was positively incredible (what I am relating in these pages is from the notes I wrote immediately after this vision had ended). We could now see a team of doctors (undoubtedly composed of those sitting on the platform in front of us) examining the subject to once again confirm he was clinically dead.

In this regard, no fewer than five tests were performed to ensure this was indeed the case. The vital sign readings were marked clearly on a blackboard in the room where the attempted revival was taking place. At the same time, we witnessed several fluids being injected into the deceased's arm. I assumed this was a massive infusion of blood.

Next, we saw a rather large machine being wheeled in and positioned directly over the man's chest and midsection. Another smaller machine was placed over his skull. The doctor explained that exactly at the moment of death (four days earlier), the individual's undamaged brain, along with his heart and several other organs, had been removed and placed into special oxygen freeze containers.

He then noted that they had later been taken out of the container prior to the start of this presentation, thawed by means of a special process and placed back into the dead man's body. It required no more than three hours to successfully accomplish this surgery.

The machine being lowered onto his skull was now continuing the body's "warming" process.

We were then told that the larger machine hovering over his chest and mid-section could restore the ends of the body's chromosomes so that they once again could be fully functional. At the same time, this incredible machine was also rejuvenating the pumping system within the heart.

I watched this whole process in utter fascination. As the device worked its magic, the doctor commented, "This, ladies and gentlemen, will become the 'machine of life.'"

As he said this, I suddenly wondered about the legal, moral, and religious implications of what I was observing. I thought to myself, wasn't resurrection God's responsibility? And, was this really the right thing to do? I recall that it was at this point that something startling happened.

The fingers of the deceased man's right hand began to move. Some of the spectators around me started to utter, oohs, ahhs, and begin to applaud.

And rightly so.

The lead doctor then confirmed that we had witnessed the successful conclusion of reviving this clinically dead individual. Moments later, even though he was still now under sedation, we could see other parts of the man's body move: his arms, his feet, and even a slight turn of his head.

The doctor then began to provide some medical history about this individual, whom he soon began addressing as his patient. He informed us that as a result of an auto accident, both of his legs, one arm, and his spine had been broken.

He told us that during the period when he was clinically dead, a renowned crack surgical team was able to repair all of these fractures using a state-of-the-art medical adhesive with no concern about losing the victim in the process. Now that he was alive, all of these repairs would continue to mend normally during the usual expected healing period and he would eventually be as good as he was before the accident.

What was plain to me was that this was not a combination of techniques and equipment. This had been one smooth operation, far different from what is being used currently in different parts of the world.

In response to the barrage of questions now being asked from those in attendance, the medical team made it clear this potential life restoration process was applicable in nearly any situation. They further surprised everyone by stating that this particular resurrection was actually the 23rd such procedure they had successfully performed.

As I sat there as part of the excited audience, my head began to swirl. I closed my eyes to try and regain my senses. Then, as fast as this had happened, I was back in my Baton Rouge hotel room.

Again, I must emphasize, I have no idea what year I had been transported to or in what medical facility all of this had taken place.

But one thing was clear. It had happened.

I had seen the dead brought back to life.

Before I end my discussion of this vision, I must emphasize that should it someday become reality, the implications of such a possibility would require us to reexamine much about who and what we are, and our everyday obligations. For example: social security and government pensions, forced retirements, the role of the church in life-and-death decisions, medical costs of resurrecting the dead, and the ability to pay the cost of continued care for the elderly, etc.

It might also be appropriate, after talking about bringing the dead back to life, to discuss society's current trend toward wanting to cause incredible harm to each other. To do so, I am jumping over a number of other visions to one that occurred in October 2013.

But first, some background.

One of my great pleasures is the study of history. This includes the days of ancient Rome, a period when gladiatorial combat was strongly indicative of its people's declining moral values. Such activities were given the term "games," which erroneously suggested that these sadistic events could be categorized as sporting activities. For the most part, they were anything but. The people wanted to see blood—and often the arena floor was covered with it.

Particularly when armed, well-trained gladiators entertained audiences by means of one-sided, violent confrontations. Some were with wild animals that were no match for the weapons and steel nets used against them, others were with condemned criminals, and defenseless Christians who usually were weak and malnourished. However, there were exceptions.

These were matches (often the most anticipated part of the day's "program") wherein unknown volunteers who had submitted to basic combat training would fight well-known, often adulated gladiators. These confrontations probably were the closest to what might be considered genuine competition, though even describing them as competitive is something of a stretch.

Why would anyone even want to place themselves in such a potentially perilous situation? Because such combat represented the shortest path to glory (and, for the most part, a viable alternative to suicide). Most of the participants in these matches risked their social standing, not to mention their lives, in their quest for popular acclaim and the financial rewards that might follow. They realized that if they were victorious, they would become instant heroes.

Nevertheless, most of these contests were also one-sided. In fact, an upset victory was a rare occurrence.

But, if these volunteers or prisoners did score such an upset and went on to do so again and again, they were often elevated to high levels in the Roman "pecking" order by no less than the Emperor himself. Some even became legends and were commemorated in story and art.

Why am I mentioning the topic of ancient Rome now? Mostly because of my concern that we as a society may be trending back to a lust for an absolute life-ending final result in one-on-one combat, particularly when I see some of the matches on television that are called Total Combat.

It is something of a combination of boxing and wrestling, fought in steel cages with rules that put the combatants at a much greater risk than either boxing or wrestling. For example, they not only allow for kicking, but in many instances seem to encourage it when one of the fighters is down. The potential for massive, even fatal bodily harm is substantial.

What worries me most is that these attractions draw huge TV audiences. Networks are well aware that their space rates for advertising are driven by the number of viewers watching at any given time. Consequently, there will be a continued effort to feed the frenzy for violence craved by those who are tuned in.

I am an old-school fan of boxing, and I have seen some of the greatest athletes who ever climbed into the ring. I had the opportunity to watch Joe Louis, Rocky Marciano, Sugar Ray Robinson, Sugar Ray Leonard, and probably the greatest of them all: Muhammad Ali (while he was still "floating like a butterfly and stinging like a bee").

But today the real, honest-to-goodness boxing idols are but fleeting memories.

Nevertheless, there still remain vestiges of traditional boxing as some of us remember it. Boxing that relies on the Marquess of Queensberry rules. In fact, in October 2013 I had the opportunity to help prepare three young fighters for upcoming bouts in Brooklyn, New York. How?

By instilling in them the utilization of "mind power" to build the confidence and skills they needed to convince them that they could be victorious. The result?

All three were winners. I am particularly proud of Heather "The Heat" Hardy whom I worked with and conditioned for what (at that point) would be the most important bout of her life. My main goal was to train her to be so alert so as to almost anticipate the blows thrown at her by her opponent and in doing so deflect them. The result made me particularly proud. On October 15, 2014, she became the WBC Junior Featherweight Champion of the World.

I bring all of this up as the possible reason for my next vision. It came a week after their victories.

VISION No. 12

The Cage of Death

After my involvement in the aforementioned boxing matches, I received substantial coverage in a number of local newspapers (as might be expected any time a mentalist is asked to successfully improve an athlete's performance). Consequently, the next day, my computer and telephone lines were flooded with congratulatory messages.

One call stood out.

The call bore a request that was strange, because the voice of the caller had a cold, bland, far-away feeling. It was from a man who claimed to be involved in the Total Combat matches and, in fact, managed such a fighter. He wondered if I could produce the same results with his client.

Considering that my time does not come without cost, and I abhorred this kind of cruel one-on-one "anything goes" combat, my instinctive reaction was to simply hang up the phone, but somehow, almost as if I was prevented from doing so, I agreed to meet him. I should point out that, immediately after doing so, I regretted my decision. Yet the compulsion that drew me to agree was eerie.

Our meeting was for the following week, which gave me enough leeway to juggle my schedule. We were to get together at a fight club in South Amboy, New Jersey. He gave me precise directions in the same bland voice—with neither emotion nor change in tone.

Still, I did not back out.

Possibly because I already had a luncheon scheduled in Atlantic City for the next day, and since South Amboy represented a mere hour-and-a-half drive from my home, I accepted. Little did I know, my next vision was to provide the reasons for my being there. Unknowingly, I had set up an appointment with someone not of this world.

The week passed quickly. And this new vision (like all the others) came without warning. One minute, I was still at home; the next, I was in front of the arena where we were supposed to meet. Actually, I was standing in a half-filled parking lot. People were walking by, paying me no attention.

As in past visions, my first concern was trying to determine where I was, and when.

Now, here is where this vision goes off on a strange tangent. Whenever I entered into one of these vision states, I was usually invisible to everyone. However, today, for some reason, a man was approaching me who had no difficulty seeing me.

Not only that, he was waving to catch my attention. I was stunned. Was this another person who, like me, could also be whisked off mysteriously to far-away places? Either that or he had to be a ghost. As it turned out, that was a pretty good guess.

He was tall, with a face that showed indentations from old scars. It was easy to see he probably once was a fighter. He appeared to be somewhere in his late 60s, which he later acknowledged (we actually were able to talk to each other). He told me he was once considered an "up-and-comer," and had headed up many preliminaries on championship cards—several in Madison Square Garden, and one at Yankee Stadium.

The only name he gave me was Doc.

Doc (ghost or no ghost) turned out to be an interesting chap (even though his expressions never changed and he seemed to always stare straight ahead). He told me that as a young man he had been considered someone to watch—possibly even a contender for the welterweight championship, but an early injury forced him to the sidelines and to eventually become a manager.

As the afternoon drifted on, I found myself enthralled with his stories of the many champions he had worked with. He was able to punctuate a few of them with numerous clippings, and even had several showing him and members of his team holding his fighters overhead after their victories.

I could see that not only had Doc been in the corner of many of the sport's greatest combatants, but according to all of the appreciative notes and letters he showed me, he enjoyed a friendship with most of them right up to the time he died (keep in mind, I was talking to a ghost). The bottom line: Doc had lived an extremely interesting life.

With all of this nostalgic boxing talk, we hardly noticed that several hours had passed. Actually, the subject I most wanted to discuss with him, Total Combat, was hardly touched upon.

But as it turned out, any further discussion was not necessary. He was soon leading me to two ringside seats, actually cage-side seats, which for some reason, had a sign on them marked "Reserved." This was the second time in mere weeks that I had occupied such a favorable vantage point--during the bouts in Brooklyn, I had also been seated right next to the action.

By now, the crowds were filing in. Doc and I sat there for approximately 15 minutes before the announcer rang a bell to start the evening's proceedings.

The fighters in the first contest were escorted into the arena amidst a blast of lights, explosions, and even bikini-clad damsels sprinkling rose petals in their path. The crowd loved it.

Immediately after they entered the cage, the announcer introduced a number of popular cage brawlers. One was a current champion. Another was a former champion. He then called several officials into the cage, which, as expected, drew some boos.

There were even a few local celebrities in attendance, mostly stand-up comics. I wondered whether he would have called me to come up if I had actually been there; and if he did, would they cheer if they knew of my negative feelings about Total Combat?

However, I did not have time to give that much thought. The arena's lights darkened and several spotlights focused on the cage. What came next, I will never forget.

Within minutes, the bell rang for the start of the match. There was a sudden flurry of hits, kicks, tosses to the canvas, neck and leg holds, and severe punches. Blood flowed from both fighters.

I hated what I was witnessing; from my point of view, this was fighting in its rawest form—but as far as Doc was concerned, this was combat as it was meant to be. By now, he was standing, eyes glazed, emotionless. Every once in a while, he would turn to look at me as if to seek my approval, but I just sat there, almost limp in my seat.

Suddenly, one of the combatants was lying still on the canvas. By his side, kneeling, were two men in white coats. One of them looked up and shook his head, indicating the fighter appeared dead. Fortunately, however, he then reversed his call, indicating that the fallen fighter was just unconscious.

But here was the incredible part: instead of the audience cheering, there was extensive booing. Exactly what you would have expected from the ancient Romans watching slaves being slaughtered in the arena. The crowd was actually throwing objects at the outer part of the cage. There seemed to be intense disappointment that the downed fighter had survived.

The ring announcer had now taken hold of the victorious fighter's arm and made the following announcement (I wrote this down later, after my vision ended): "Ladies and gentlemen, by virtue of inflicting a near-life-ending blow to his opponent in one minute and 22 seconds in the third round, the winner is (name purposely deleted)."

Nearby, I could hear the blow-by-blow radio announcer telling of the fans' great disappointment in not seeing a fight-to-the-death conclusion to this ugly match.

I sat there, shocked. Had our value of life descended to such a low? Was having the match end with one of its participants surviving actually a disappointment to the crowd? Was this cage I was staring at a modern-day version of the arena in which gladiators fought helpless slaves in ancient Rome?

Unfortunately, that was my conclusion.

I remained seated in the midst of all this bloodlust, with crowds cheering and clapping, and screaming the winner's name. I wondered what insane year this was. Doc was no longer at my side. In fact, he was completely gone. Beneath my feet was a discarded sports section from a newspaper.

Its date: Feb 16, 2018. I then realized I had witnessed an event three years into the future.

I want to again stress that I am not a psychic. I am a flesh-and-bones human being with greatly enhanced mental, perceptive, and intuitive powers that are accompanied by the ability to know what people are thinking. During this incredible vision experience, it appeared obvious that the man called Doc was a ghost. I have many opinions about ghosts and the hereafter, but this is not the place to discuss them. I will just say that this was the first time a ghost entered one of my visions.

Later that night, the blood and gore I had witnessed lingered in my mind. It was still there the following day. So much so, that while driving toward my Atlantic City appointment, I felt the need to stop at a rest stop to throw up. Someone in the restroom asked me if I was OK. I told him I was not.

How terribly discouraging it was to look ahead and discover we will have arrived at a point where death in a sporting event would be the ultimate thrill. And anything less than DEATH would be a disappointment to the paying audience. I hope with all my heart that this vision fails to come true.

(NOTE: I gave this vision priority because it did not happen during the past few years, it occurred recently. It also made me again speculate whether my own activities, the specific places I visit, or even the news stories I see on TV, could possibly be the stimuli for potential visions. If so, then the one I just described most likely would have been caused by my having worked with the three young boxers in Brooklyn.)

Usually, in any particular year, I travel tens of thousands of miles, and this requires my use of just about every form of transportation. Much of this crisscrossing of America is accomplished by plane or train taking me as close as possible to my next scheduled appearance. From there, it is usually Kreskin—behind the wheel of a rental car.

The positives of this are that I not only gain the chance to see more of this great country, but I also have an opportunity to stop at roadside restaurants or even drive into small towns and chat with some of the local people. I always find this to be an enjoyable experience. It is also educational, because each area of our country is different. The food is different. The way people talk is different. The music is different. And in many instances, even people's perspectives of how the nation is being run are different.

Nevertheless, there is one common strain in every part of this country, and it is the inherent goodness of Americans. It is constant, and it runs deep.

Throughout the pages of this book, I have touched upon my ongoing concern as to what brings on my visions. I repeat, I have undergone many medical and psychological tests. In every instance, other than normal age-related issues, I am in excellent health.

Consequently, in the case of the vision I am about to describe, I can only cite my constant driving as its possible cause. Or perhaps it was just the conversation I had with the agent at a large car rental facility.

Actually, it was routine. He had gone over all of the required legal jargon as to whether I wanted certain forms of excess insurance (which I routinely decline), but it was his description of the features of the 2014 luxury car I had rented that stuck in my mind. It had so many more technological capabilities than the cars I had driven just starting out in my career.

Somehow, because I am an entertainer who often appears on television, I am expected to move about in something that is extremely lavish, but that is not the case at all. The truth is, I was brought up with the understanding that cars serve but one purpose: transportation. I have since modified my opinion somewhat.

Still, I remember clearly, when I was a kid, there were many pre-World War II cars on the roads. In fact, my dad would tell me stories of how he used to crank up his 1936 Ford in order to get it started. Sometimes the family would actually give it a substantial push to help it along. He also told me that radios and heaters were considered extras. Blankets were always kept on hand for passengers.

Yet here I was, about to take possession of a vehicle that came equipped with all the latest and most desirable 21st-century accessories. For example, the car I was renting had such state-of-the-art equipment as a 360-degree dashboard-mounted back-up collision intervention screen, push-button gear selection, pulsating devices in the driver's seat to warn of oncoming cars or impending hazards, a parking assist system, and much more. I could hardly help wondering what auto makers might include next.

Little did I realize I was soon to find out.

VISION No. 13

Cars That Control You

<hr>

The short drive from the airport in Orlando to an inn just a few miles from International Drive was pleasant. This place was always a favorite stop of mine; the rooms were large, they offered a generous breakfast, and it was quieter than most of the other hotels that were closer to the two leading tourist attractions, Disney World and Universal Studios. I was there to discuss a future appearance on behalf of an auto manufacturer.

As I unpacked, I instinctively turned on the room's TV. Funny thing, the first picture to pop onto its screen pertained to a car commercial. Somehow, cars seemed to be catching my attention from every direction. Strange, inasmuch as there are so many more important things going on in this world.

Little did I know, fate was laying the groundwork for my next vision.

I had hardly made myself comfortable when it happened. Yes, here it was happening again: that same sensation to which I had by now become so accustomed. I immediately realized I was being transported to another date, time, and place. As usual, there was no way to resist. Once again, I was a captive time traveler.

Within nanoseconds, I arrived. I found myself in a place far different from any of my many other destinations.

I found myself surrounded by cars, cars, and more cars. They were everywhere. It was obvious I had been transported into the middle of some huge convention where automobiles were the centerpiece. Fortunately, I soon realized why.

This was not an ordinary show devoted to cars for the everyday driver. This obviously was an automobile show intended only for law enforcement professionals; there appeared to be representatives from various crime fighting agencies from around the world.

How could I be so sure? Quite simply, there was a huge banner overhead, proclaiming this 12th day in March 2018, the beginning of International Automated Car Control Week.

What was this all about? I wondered why automated control of a car warranted a gathering such as this. Whatever the reason, the hall was packed. There appeared to be many police officers in attendance, and judging from their gold braids and badges, most were of a high level. Furthermore, their uniforms indicated some were from other countries.

As usual, I was there in spectral form only. I could see everybody and everything, but once again, they could not see me. As I made my way toward what appeared to be a demonstration stage, a nearby clock indicated that the next presentation was scheduled to begin in approximately three minutes. That was fine by me. I just wanted to know what kind of demonstration they were referring to.

People were starting to gather around the stage. On its platform was what appeared to be a car covered with a tarpaulin. At exactly the announced starting time, a man boldly pulled it off. What he revealed was a car unlike anything I had seen in my time: a combination sedan and recreation vehicle, but lower and more streamlined. Protruding from its roof were what appeared to be several small fin-like attachments.

After some brief opening comments, he pointed to a large screen suddenly alive with action. What we were seeing was a video featuring the car on the platform moving along a multi-lane highway.

He then pointed out that this vehicle had been created solely for the purposes of this demonstration, and also indicated that the person at the wheel was a trained stunt driver who was instructed to initiate whatever maneuvers necessary to avoid being apprehended by law enforcement.

In this situation, "law enforcement" consisted of two vehicles and a helicopter. The stunt driver swerved, weaved, and even dipped into an embankment briefly, but the many rocks there forced him back on the road. At times, the car's speed exceeded 90 miles an hour.

The police were actually catching up. It was at that point that a patrolman in each car leaned out of its passenger side window, pistols drawn. All of a sudden, the automobile they were pursuing pulled over to the side of the road; its engine dead, its driver with no place to go.

It was at this moment that the moderator told us what we were watching was the "car that controlled you."

Those words immediately caught my attention. How could a car control you? I was soon given the answer.

"Ladies and gentlemen," the man said, "as you know, Congress has passed, and the President has signed, the new Law Enforcement Vehicle Control Act. This new legislation has mandated that auto manufacturers build into their cars remote electronics that enable local, state and federal officials to literally take control of any vehicle being pursued or has been identified as possibly having been involved in a felony."

I already was aware of illegal methods whereby hackers could plant devices into a car that could enable them to control your vehicle. But what I was hearing now, was that law enforcement could now LEGALLY do the same thing.

My initial thought as the audience applauded was, "Whoa!" A knee-jerk reaction. I then thought, "Isn't this just another intrusion by the government into the public's right to enjoy the fruits of their labors?"

My mind soon registered a firm YES. However, my weighing of the pros and cons of this issue was promptly interrupted.

The moderator soon began to reel off the many crime-fighting features of this automobile. As he did, he positioned himself next to the car on the exhibit. Remember, the people in the audience were all members of various law enforcement agencies, some even top secret. It was plain to see they were observing and listening to everything.

"Ladies and gentlemen, these are the newly mandated accessories that will soon be on most of the cars you will find in showrooms across America. Although many of them will elevate driving to a new level of enjoyment, they will also play an important role in highway law enforcement. The good news is that in most instances, they will become standard equipment."

Then he went on to describe what they were. The list was long, and utilizing my enhanced memory, I was able to later put them into my notes upon my return to my Orlando room. Here is the methodology that would one day be built into practically every car on the road: The means to remotely…

Allow all conversations within your car to be monitored and recorded, all without your knowledge;

Lock all your doors and windows, effectively leaving you a prisoner in your own car;

Detect the presence of any kind of weapon, legal or illegal;

Take control of your car and stop it or drive it to any desired destination, regardless of whether you committed any kind of legal infraction;

To secretly photograph all of the vehicle's occupants;

To lock your seat belts so that they would become restraining belts; and

To render cell phones useless except for incoming messages from law enforcement.

These were the seven that I considered the most disturbing (one might even call them the "Seven Future Sins of Governmental Intrusion into Our Driving Privileges"). After I observed this presentation, I wondered about the legal ramifications of what I had just witnessed. And since these modifications were mandatory, how much would they add to the purchase price of a new 2018 automobile?

In a sense, I wished I had not been in an invisible form. There was so much I would have liked to ask. So many points I would have liked to raise. So many objections I would have liked to put forth.

However, I have little doubt if I had been able to become visible and voice my concerns, I am certain I would not have received a great deal of support from the members of the law enforcement establishment. Deep down, I was certain they were cheering all these features.

Eventually, my vision ended, and I was left to my thoughts.

I realized such changes in our vehicles were being introduced in the name of law and order. But was this overkill?

Frankly, there are few of us who are actually criminals. So few of us who would require such unfair treatment. So few of us who would not stop at the sight of a flashing light behind us. I wondered if there had not been more going on in their introduction than met the eye. In fact, were the controls over the people in our country being purposefully drawn tighter?

My mind kept flashing a disturbing answer: YES!

VISION No. 14

Faster Than Fast

———— ⟪⟫ ————

Visions of travel continued to occupy my thoughts. It was just a few weeks after my automobile experience when I began thinking in terms of another form of transportation, a flight to England.

I had received word from my agent that there was some interest in having me travel to Britain for some demonstrations, even a possible theatrical run. Nothing had yet been firmed up. Still, such an opportunity was exciting to contemplate.

It had been quite a while since I performed in England, and I remember having enjoyed it immensely, but blocking out enough time for such a trip might be very difficult.

Too bad. Not enough days, weeks, or months to do all the things I want to do. (NOTE: Nor are there enough days, weeks, or months to do all the things I have *committed* to do.)

The truth is, time seems to be my number-one adversary. Somehow I always find myself seeking more of it, and it is an ongoing quest, given the life I live. Unfortunately, my days begin early and my nights end late. In between, there are meetings, phone calls, messages to respond to, performances and, after all of that, countless trips to airports.

Ah, airports! Not only is it difficult getting to them, but then there is parking, checking in, going through the inspections, and the endless waiting at the gate (only to be rewarded by frequent flight cancellations).

It was at one of these gates that I become fixated on the many large jets taxiing to and fro, preparing for either an arrival or departure. That was when I realized how seldom I take the time to truly consider what an accomplishment commercial flight really is. Actually, these aircraft are as close to technological miracles as mankind has ever conceived.

I began to think back to a long-ago history teacher instilling in my mind the place where aviation had its birth. He did an effective job, because I have never forgotten that it all began in Kitty Hawk, North Carolina. The date: December 17, 1903. Its initiators: two bicycle shop owners, Wilbur and Orville Wright.

In my mind, I could almost picture their frail, lovingly constructed, kite-like creation rolling down its makeshift runway, and then slowly rising a few feet off the ground until it accomplished what, until then, was considered virtually impossible: sustained flight by a heavier-than-air machine.

To observers, it must have looked more like a Rube Goldberg contraption. But it worked, and in two indelible ways; the first was that it would soon make the world a much smaller place, and the second was that the airplane became a potent weapon.

After this introduction, the floodgates of piloted flight widened significantly. By World War I, airplanes had been fully assimilated into mankind's arsenal of weaponry. More importantly, they also assimilated into a prime means of long-distance transportation. They became *airlines*, transporting passengers faster and more easily than anyone had ever thought possible.

However, it was the next step that became the forefront of aviation. Jet travel, which was to evolve into the next major event in aviation history: the moon landing of Apollo 11 in 1969. At last, mankind's attention was finally focused on the full potential of jet-powered flight.

While regular passenger excursions to the moon have yet to become a reality, jet power has continued to make significant strides forward. One such achievement has been in the ability of planes to whisk people across the Atlantic in approximately three and a half hours.

Yes, I said three and a half hours. Not the customary seven and a half. This spectacular feat of air travel was occurring on a regular basis in 1967 via the Concorde. The flight time of this sleekly designed, needle-like supersonic aircraft was half the normal seven hours still required by commercial jets. While you would think the world would immediately and continuously embrace this incredible experience, such was not the case. As it turned out, there were too many problems along the way.

Sadly, in the late stages of its nearly three-decade career, the Concorde's owners were forced to raise its fares due to several key factors, most notably the increased cost of fuel and large-scale cutbacks on international executives traveling via supersonic transport regularly. Consequently, its profitability started to dip into the red.

That was just the beginning: new, more stringent FAA requirements for high-altitude supersonic jets necessitated a massive updating of various onboard navigational and communication systems. To make matters worse, many of its most potentially profitable destinations were not accessible due to the short length of their runways.

However, the final feather plucked from the Concorde's wings was the mounting number of complaints against the thunderous noise the big bird created. Whole communities in and around New York and Washington, D.C. made their protests heard loud and clear. It eventually became a politically charged issue that was to ground this amazing airplane permanently. Ultimately, the Concorde was retired in 2003 after 27 years of mostly profitable service.

Now we sit in the year 2015, still relying on conventional jet planes to carry us to distant destinations. My next vision told me such carriers were about to undergo another startling change.

It was a remarkable vision, and began in the same manner as most of the others, only this one was to originate in Washington's Dulles airport. One minute I was sitting at my airport gate waiting to board a flight to New Jersey, and the next, I was in a far different place.

Once again, the transition happened suddenly; this time, I seemed to have been transported to a line in a huge waiting area in a strange airport. I could see that I had somehow jumped years into the future, but I had no idea exactly where I was.

I could determine that I was among a group that was about to be escorted up a ramp and into a craft that appeared to be right out of a science fiction movie.

As it turned out, I was entering the largest airplane I had ever seen, was easily the size of three present-day 747s laid out end to end. Its width was approximately twice that of a jumbo jet.

As usual, I was invisible to everyone around me. I joined the crowd entering the cavernous interior of this massive airship, and we were greeted by a welcoming voice over the speaker system. While it had a very officious tone, it also obviously and carefully been chosen to convey a feeling of both confidence and strength by its creators and builders (identified as two well-known aircraft designers, one located in France, and the other in the U.S.).

He welcomed us aboard the airship's initial flight and described the plane as an SBJ (a Supersonic Business Jet). He jokingly referred to it as the fully developed, "well-educated son" of the Concorde that he had nicknamed "Big John," but offspring that now was much quieter, much faster, and much more comfortable than the SST. He also added that it was much less costly to put in the air. If he was right, Big John would probably change the definition of jet travel.

Our attention was then directed to the plush, comfortable interior of this massive airship. It offered built-in sound capabilities, individual temperature control zones, and television from all parts of the world.

He pointed out that there was only one class in this craft. He called it "Exalted

Luxury Class" which seemed like a description no one would dare dispute. He next informed us that the distance between seats provided for one entire foot of legroom more than in conventional airplanes.

There were several other cabin features that he felt worthy of extra attention: individual passenger monitors that provided in-flight access to any television channel in the world, and cabin pressure capabilities and temperature controls that would allow the ship to reach an altitude of 50,000 feet or more with passengers experiencing no discomfort whatsoever.

My heightened perceptive abilities alerted me to a mounting excitement in the crowd. I soon learned the reason why. The voice now invited us each to choose any seat at random. The group only numbered about 100, a fraction of the number of available seats. I now suspected we were about to be taken for a ride.

And I was right.

Next came the expected "fasten your seatbelts" announcement, but with one added comment: "Ladies and gentlemen, you are about to embark on a trip you will never forget." With these few words, we began rolling down the runway. Minutes later we had taken off.

Once in the air, I could now see where I had been. Below was the capital of the United States. I had to look fast, because in what appeared to be a mere instant, we were soaring over what had to be the Atlantic Ocean. In less than 30 minutes, the voice instructed us to prepare for a landing. It was smooth. It was uneventful. And its destination was a wonderful surprise.

Outside the cabin windows was an azure blue sky and swaying palm trees. We had landed in Bermuda.

Imagine, Bermuda in less than half an hour!

We were then invited to disembark. Again, more comforts. This magnificent craft contained four more doors than present-day airplanes, all leading to an expanded ramp. Clearly, high priority had been given to passenger comfort as still another aspect of the plane's superior design.

The pleasures of this excursion were to continue. Once again, we found ourselves in a large passenger area, where, to everyone's delight, another surprise was waiting: a huge buffet table filled with a marvelous assortment of food choices. Unfortunately, my state of invisibility precluded my being able to drink or eat anything. Especially regrettable, because the lobster appeared to be delectable, most likely caught fresh off the shore of this pearl of an island.

After sufficient time had been allowed for everyone to have their fill of food and drink, our up-to-now-hidden spokesman made his appearance.

His stature pretty much matched his voice. He was wearing a business suit and introduced himself as a member of the corporate management team responsible for this *wondercraft*.

I began to suspect that we were about to experience a well-prepared commercial presentation. It turned out my guess was correct. I soon learned two very important pieces of information. The first was that the people around me consisted of reporters from various business media outlets, and the other was that the spectacular machine that flew us here had done so at a speed exceeding Mach 3 (or approximately 2,200 miles per hour).

At this rate of speed, the craft could transport passengers from New York to Paris in less than two hours, or from New York to various cities in Australia in five hours.

Inasmuch as my visions do not allow for me to carry along any physical items, I could not record all the technical specifications he was spelling out for the acutely attentive members of aviation and business media. But later, reading my notes, I noticed I had indicated that our "short" hop between Washington, D.C., and Bermuda, a distance of 825 miles, was covered in less than a half an hour.

It was certainly not a trip to Paris in two hours or to Australia in five hours, but, the creators of this magnificent aircraft had made their point. I had also noted the year of our arrival (as indicated on the Arrivals and Departures Schedule Board date of arrival in the Bermuda reception area) as being in the year as 2019.

How marvelous it is to contemplate that in just a mere five years we will be soaring through the air to practically any destination at three times the speed of sound. I also wonder how costly such supersonic travel will be; without a doubt, it will be much more than travelers paid for travel on the Concorde before it retired.

I should also note, my return to our present date (to keep this description in aviation terms) was a smooth landing: one minute I was standing amidst the group in Bermuda, and the next, I was back in the year 2014 at my gate at Dulles Airport.

But I did arrive back in my own unique manner, and with lots of food for thought. Needless to repeat, these sudden transitions continue to remain mysterious. Some still even leaving me feeling weak and occasionally sick. Yet others bring me back feeling perfect, and in some instances actually invigorated. This vision had been a trip with the latter result.

In retrospect, I have no solid explanation for why I was caught up in this event, except that it simply happened. Possibly, it was the result of my mind having been stimulated by the magnificent planes visible from the gate window. I may have been dispatched to the year 2019 for no other reason than to observe and report to the world what awaits it. If so, I sincerely hope I have achieved both goals.

As for the year 2019, I will be looking forward to someday actually traveling on that massive airship. Until then, one thought keeps dancing in my mind: New York to Paris between breakfast and lunch, wow!

VISION No.15

Through a Door to "Anywhere"

———⋅⟨∞⟩⋅———

I felt this next vision was a good follow-up to the one I just described (and it happened just a short while later).

Through the years, I have had a fascination with virtual reality. This is a method that enables a person using certain state-of-the-art technology to be transported to a completely different setting, be it a mythical place, another country, or even a far-off planet. There are practically no limits whatsoever.

Usually, the experience requires the wearing of a helmet, special glasses, and a large viewing screen, the larger, the better. With such equipment, users are able to interact with various programs that potentially cast them into the midst of whatever is going on within their view.

Young people, in particular, welcome such an experience because it possibly puts them into their video games side by side with superheroes, or fiendish monsters on a mission to devour the world, or aliens determined to capture the planet Earth.

Up to now, the combination of helmet, glasses, and computer equipment has done a pretty good job of meeting the needs of virtual reality participants, with one exception: the ability to experience the sensation of personal maneuverability. Currently, game participants can only stand, aim, and shoot. They can see enemies falling all around them, hear screams, and practically feel explosions—but they are unable to enjoy the thrill of pursuing the enemy.

It seems that this missing dimension of today's virtual reality experience may soon be overcome by means of several inventions taking shape here and in Europe. The most popular among these is an actual support frame, similar to what can be found in a child's baby stroller. This device harnesses participants to allow their feet to walk on an attached platform without falling. Observers believe it should satisfy players' immediate goals.

Is it the ultimate prize in maximizing the virtual reality experience? I am now convinced it is not. Why?

Because I was about to experience in my next vision that true virtual reality really is just around the corner.

It is a rare night that I can actually spend back at my home in New Jersey. I was relaxing while watching an old episode of *Star Trek*. Admittedly, I am not a hardcore fan, but I do admire the thinking and imagination that has gone into the show. In most instances, I am drawn to the Starship Enterprise's virtual reality room, which, as many devoted fans know, often plays a key part in the program's weekly episodes.

Still, I want to emphasize that what I experienced was not a dream, nor did it have anything to do with *Star Trek* or space travel; no, it had everything to do with a combination of science and a form of relaxation that will eventually become commonplace, which, from my point of view, is a combination I always enjoy.

One thing is for sure: I came away from this vision convinced that true virtual reality will become a marvelous addition to our future.

This latest excursion began with a sudden transition to a place among a group of what I soon realized were scientists, researchers, special feature writers, and teachers. I was in an auditorium. On its stage were several men and a woman.

Through the windows on the sides of the room I could see trees, and down below were what appeared to be students. It was obvious I was on a college campus. As I looked around, I noticed many of those in attendance carrying some kind of program.

On its cover was the date in large letters: JUNE 9, 2017.

As I stood there staring at the stage, the only woman among the seated group stood up to speak. She introduced herself as a scientist and PhD graduate of a well-known New England school, part of a team working on behalf of a public company involved in virtual reality research.

(NOTE: Throughout this book, I have made a point of not mentioning names of specific individuals or the companies with whom they are associated, simply because most of my visions take place in the future. Consequently, some of the people and companies described in these visions may not yet have been involved with the events or developments disclosed. To make such additional information public now might result in advance speculation in the companies or bothersome publicity to the people involved.)

On a table in front of this woman were what appeared to be helmets. I watched and listened intently.

She picked one up and remarked that as recently as several years earlier (probably in our current time, 2015), this helmet could achieve what most people considered a stunning breakthrough; but in reality, it was nothing more than a glorified video game.

She stated, "With built-in fold-down glasses, its wearer could enter a world to do anything, be anyplace, and feel any sensation. But it had its limitations. It depended on individual programs."

She gave numerous examples of how people used the technology. "For instance, its wearers could singlehandedly defeat armies, become Supermen with X-ray vision, or transform into winning quarterbacks or home run kings. And more."

"For all perceived purposes," she continued, "its users could experience a sense of omnipotence beyond belief within the unlimited realm of whatever specific gaming experience they chose."

From my point of view, the helmets looked almost as large as those worn by astronauts. Each seemed to be adorned with what appeared to be diodes or some kind of external connectors to accommodate some sort of necessary wiring.

It was obvious, for all practical reasons, they were clumsy. The speaker continued, "But now virtual reality is about to advance by leaps and bounds."

As we all wondered how, she quickly answered her own question.

"Ladies and gentlemen, by virtue of various kinds of stimuli, either self-imposed, or powered into the minds of the wearers, any environment or situation they imagine can become real enough to be interacted with. This, my friends, is self-imposed mind control. And without any kind of external equipment."

Bingo! She had finally hit my nerve button.

For years, I have been practicing my own personal mind control. I always used it judiciously. Specifically, when simple diversions such as TV or reading were not enough, I would simply make happen all the things she was now suggesting others might now accomplish and without a helmet.

And I was able to do so by using my own mental abilities. I can assure you, every time I called upon these skills to create my own virtual reality happening, it was a fantastic experience. Now, if you believed what the speaker was saying, this same ability might soon be close at hand for everyone.

The group was instructed to form a line and follow the speaker to what appeared to be a small square vestibule. Inasmuch as I was invisible to everyone around me, I jumped in line behind the nearest person.

As each attendee moved forward toward this small edifice, I noticed there was another scientist standing at its entrance, briefly whispering something into each person's ear as they walked by. I could hardly wait to hear what it was. Happily, it took but a few minutes until the man in front of me reached the area where the scientist was standing.

Her instructions were to "Imagine any place you would like to be right now, then walk through the vestibule and through the next door in front of you."

I anxiously followed the person I was standing behind. Within seconds, I was through the additional door. Inside was a sign that read:

"YOU ARE ONLY PERMITTED TO STAY FOR THREE MINUTES.
YOU WILL HEAR YOUR NAME ANNOUNCED WHEN YOUR TIME IS UP."

Once inside, I was surprised to find a large room and many of the men and women who had already entered. Overhead, I could hear speakers softly announcing names of those who were now being told it was their time to leave. It was obvious that few, if any, wanted to leave. Each had found their personal "Eden." In fact, some of the people were making audible pleas to remain longer. But to no avail.

From side doors (as if out of nowhere), came what appeared to be "ushers." They politely escorted those whose names had been called through another door that led back to the original auditorium.

As I observed those still in this mysterious room, I had little doubt that whatever virtual reality they were now part of was the embodiment of their utmost desires. Many were smiling, talking, and waving their arms. Whatever they said or did, it was not noticed by anyone around them, each was lost in their own self-imposed dream state, and enjoying it immensely. It was a strange sight, almost as if I was watching a choreographed exhibition of solo dancers.

However, by now, I had a more important mission; I had to find out how these men and women could experience a virtual reality transition without a helmet or personal wiring. I was convinced that somehow, in some manner, their minds were being programmed by highly advanced computer circuits built into this room.

By the time the name of the original person I had followed was called, I felt I might as well leave also. I had had enough time to study my surroundings. The room seemed bereft of visible wiring, strange lights, or anything else that could serve as conduits for the transmission of any kind of mental impulses.

I have to admit, my skills do not overflow into advanced computer technology, so I had little choice but to leave and hope that the explanation we would be given would be suitable to fill in the gaps.

It had been an incredible event. My only regret was that I was not there in flesh-and-blood form, so I could have physically and mentally experienced the true capability of what appeared to be a fascinating new technology.

Back in the auditorium, by a show of hands, everyone indicated they had gone through the virtual reality experience. They were talking and laughing, many were still shaking their heads in amazement. It was obvious that this startling visitation into an *impossible* realm had impressed them beyond their expectations. In a matter of minutes, they made their pleasure known with a standing ovation for the team of scientists.

Once more, the speaker stood up, thanked everyone, and then motioned for the audience to be seated. She began her follow-up by providing the information I was waiting for.

However, I soon realized I would be disappointed because her explanation was filled with the kind of scientific details that those in attendance feasted on.

Keep in mind, these were all people whose careers (in one way or another) were deeply rooted in science. Accordingly, they scrupulously took notes, recorded every word spoken, and photographed each of the speakers. She and the members of the scientific team obliged by crossing as many "t's" and dotting as many "i's" as possible, and also took questions from the audience. Here are just a few of the most important ones.

Question: Might such virtual reality rooms or chambers be set up in key locations so that they could be utilized by anyone?
Answer: Yes, but their best use will be in various aspects of psychological therapy.

Question: But can a doctor, using this technology with a patient, be able to monitor the specific reality scene his patient ventures into?
Answer: As of now, no.

Question: Is there any method being worked on to allow another person, such as a doctor, to enter the same virtual reality experience of another human being?
Answer: Yes, but it is far from being at an operational stage.

Question: Are there any limits as to what a person's mind might produce once inside?
Answer: No.

As might be expected, the question-and-answer session went on for over an hour. It remained fascinating.

My knowledge of the various sciences was hardly on a level with those asking the questions, and furthermore, I did not have any physical abilities to either write or utilize any recording device in my current state. I was just there in a "spirit-like" invisible form. Therefore, I could only listen and attempt to grasp the full essence of what was being said.

Then, as if nothing had occurred, it was over. Not just the question-and-answer period, but everything. I was suddenly back at my home in New Jersey.

As usual, nothing in the room had changed, and the bedside clock indicated practically no time had passed.

Nevertheless, without hesitation, I felt compelled to write down everything I could remember from this startling experience.

In essence, I indicated that by the year 2017 the long-awaited virtual reality breakthrough will occur. Science will be able to release the mind's capability to inhabit one's imagination without further need for a technologically loaded, digitally reinforced, glasses-equipped helmet or any other kind of external equipment.

However, it remained obvious this improved technology still was encumbered by one very significant limitation: participants could only experience the wonder of virtual reality while influenced by the force fields built into the walls of the specific rooms, such as the one I journeyed through. And these rooms would probably be accessible only in hospitals, clinics, rest facilities, or possibly even amusement parks offering virtual reality "journeys" and charging a significant fee to enter.

Regrettably, it will probably be years before commercial companies might be permitted to construct such rooms as part of future homes. But it definitely will happen; when it does, they will function as an incredible portal to free the human mind to venture in any direction it desires.

I feel well qualified to make such a statement because, as I indicated earlier, I have been able to direct my own mind into virtual reality experiences for years— whenever and wherever I have felt a need to do so.

VISION NO. 16

Controlling the "Force"

Earlier in this book, I emphasized that I hardly consider myself another Nostradamus, and I do not mean to resurrect such a comparison now. I simply am who I am. Who that is will be for you to judge.

Yet at one point in his life, even Nostradamus must have thought of himself as being normal, at least until that day when he too must have realized he was "different." Profoundly different.

I wonder when that realization took place. How did he feel? How did Nostradamus learn to live with his special gifts?

I remember what went through my mind. The experience is as real to me today as it was then.

What might surprise you is that it was not a happy time. I was a mere age 8 1/2 when *my awakening* came, and I kept fluctuating between confusion, fright, and pure loneliness. In every other way, though, I was just like any youngster of my age; but unlike them, I began to know things in advance. I began to know things that other kids did not, could not—and *should not* know.

For example, when the telephone was about to ring, when a visitor was about to knock at our door, where lost items could be found, I already *knew*.

My family was bewildered.

Teachers were concerned.

Classmates, on the other hand? Well, they were impressed.

To make matters worse, when word got around that, "This kid's doing the *impossible*," most people thought I was using outside assistance to produce these extraordinary results; of course they thought this, I wasn't even 9 years old.

I certainly knew I was not receiving any outside assistance. Why didn't they?

Needless to say, I was completely in the dark as to how I was able to accomplish what was being considered impossible. At times, I thought something must be wrong with me. Little did I know I had been given a gift of extraordinary possibilities. Still, I spent many nights frightened and confused. I kept thinking over and over, "Why me?"

There were no ready answers.

But these strange abilities not only stayed with me throughout my schoolboy years, they grew progressively stronger as I matured, with more impressive capabilities revealing themselves with each passing year.

Yet, this was not to be compared to the dark ages of alchemy; I neither possessed Nostradamus' affinity for science, nor his knowledge of alchemy or of the planets. What's more, I owned no crystal ball, or anything else that might be considered basic tools of someone who could predict the future.

Also unlike Nostradamus, who seemingly had no inhibitions in making his extraordinary talents known, I continued to play mine down. Even when, in addition to sensing things before they occurred, I began to have the first of what would be my occasional visions.

They alarmed me in the beginning; however, I soon was able to get used to them, even when they included what appeared to be important happenings.

I mean *profoundly* important happenings.

For instance, during the World War II years (yes, I do go back that far), in one such vision I was standing on a curb in the street as a gaggle of soldiers and horses passed by. People were crying and commenting how much they loved Franklin Delano Roosevelt.

As it turned out, he actually died four months later.

Yes, I foresaw that happening; and as I grew older, I envisioned the explosion of the atomic bomb, the Berlin Wall, the Korean War, and many other important events. Still, I told no one.

All the while, my interest and fascination with the paranormal increased. Consequently, I decided to feed my pre-cognitive ability in whatever way possible: I read, I traveled, I inquired, I listened, and I experimented.

I also found myself drawn to anything that appeared to be impossible, most of which was achieved by stage magicians. Even though I do not like to be put in the same category as a magician, I always loved magic shows. Their miracles were accomplished by performers adept both in sleight of hand and sleight of mind. I watched how audiences applauded and gasped in amazement after each demonstration of the impossible.

I began to realize that most of the amazement they achieved was with gimmicked boxes, mirrors, attractive assistants, and misdirection – results I could accomplish unassisted, using only the power of my mind. I was already doing this with friends and family in the privacy of my own home.

That is when I began to entertain the ramifications of taking my powers beyond my closed doors. Was the world really ready to see miracles accomplished in a miraculous way?

Needless to say, the "GO" sign lit up in my mind. The result of which is a 60-plus-year career.

I am tempted to use the phrase, "the rest is history," but it is hardly the case. In fact, it was many years before I experienced real success. Not only as a stage performer, but also as a lecturer, consultant, and someone who could truly teach effective methods of mind control. This was helped along when I was able to utilize my acute skills of perception to actually interpret people's thoughts.

Again, I want to point out, this was not achieved by artificial means or by use of confederates in the audience; consequently, critics and the general public were now seeing me as someone who could also read minds—a major boost to my reputation. Fortunately, the word soon began to spread. I was now perceived as "a performer to watch," someone who could actually know what people were thinking. In essence, accomplishing what generally was considered *impossible*.

As a result, the demands for my services were increasing.

But the big step forward was when my name Kreskin evolved to that of THE AMAZING KRESKIN.

Soon, emcees and hosts of nighttime TV shows began referring to Kreskin being to mentalism what Houdini was to escapes. To me, this was a high compliment. But, something else new and exciting was entering my life: I was suddenly and unexpectedly beginning to receive my very first vision experiences. As I have indicated elsewhere in this book, their arrival was often frightening, constantly out of the blue—and always startling.

Needless to say this new dimension of my mysterious talents again made me wonder, "Why me? Why was I gifted with these strange abilities?"

Unfortunately, this question remains unanswered. Nevertheless, I soon found myself actually looking forward to the onset of these happenings. Their incredible realism and profound accuracy became thrilling to contemplate.

Yet, through all of my attempts to understand how these visions actually occurred, I began to realize I was also receiving a certain "other" kind of vision, a kind that might possibly provide a clue as to how others were able to part the curtains of the future. Particularly Leonardo da Vinci, whose descriptions of some of the most complex inventions of the 20th and 21st centuries had captured my attention from the time I was in a young boy.

Why Leonardo?

Because his explanations and drawings were so detailed that modern-day engineers could use them to create actual working models of the devices he had depicted. To me, it seemed near impossible for him to have been able to demonstrate such advanced perceptions of future science in what in essence were the dark ages. I was convinced that somehow, some way, he had to be receiving some mysterious, possibly even divine inspiration.

No matter how often I tried to come up with potential answers how he knew the things he set forth in his writings and illustrations, I simply could not arrive at any kind of solution.

That is—until I had the first of my very different kind of visions.

How different?

It seems none of my early visions transferred me to the future. None cast me among other people. Typically, I would find myself seated and alone in a plain room containing only what appeared to be a large window, almost like a flat television screen.

In actuality, I was not alone. There was always a voice from an invisible presence that described what I was to see or what I was about to hear. It never displayed emotion, never got louder or softer, and was always the same speaker. There always seemed to be a reason for my being "summoned."

After several such experiences, I began to truly understand what that reason might be.

I was simply to be an observer, almost as if I was carefully placed in the front row of some great theatrical epic. Why?

Possibly to be a witness to some new methodology to overcome a problem, or even a new way to conquer a problem that we in our own time had not yet mastered.

I soon wondered, could this have been the way da Vinci had been able to "envision" so many inventions not yet possible in the 15th century? Perhaps.

But why me?

Leonardo was a man of science, a man who studied the heavens, a profound thinker, and a masterful artist—someone who could clearly illustrate the incredible marvels that entered this mind.

I am neither a scientist nor an artist. Yet somehow, for some reason, I was now privy to these strange glimpses into how the future might resolve our problems. As I indicated, there were many such glimpses of wonders yet to happen.

(NOTE: I am currently contemplating working with a scientific illustrator to have my notes relating to these incidents transferred into a graphic context. This will enable them to be studied in depth as to their feasibility and potential for possible development. Hopefully, my somewhat unscientific descriptions can provide sufficient detail to make such development a practical possibility.)

Because of the recent increase in worldwide meteorological events, I have decided to provide one such example of what was revealed to me as a future solution to a deadly reoccurring problem.

This time, the voice I had heard so often was calmly telling me that I was about to be exposed to methods that might not only significantly reduce damage caused by hurricanes, but possibly even eliminate them at their point of origin.

My immediate reaction to what I had been told was reactive disbelief.

The elimination of hurricanes? Could this be?

I found myself staring intently at the large window in front of me. If what I was just told could truly be achieved, this would be a huge step forward in mankind's ongoing battle against these dreaded storms.

Furthermore, as a New Jersey resident whose friends and neighbors have sustained substantial losses of life and property due to some of America's most ferocious storms, I am keenly aware of their potential to deliver death and destruction.

Those of us living on the Eastern seaboard of the United States have become increasingly vigilant as to the awful potential results of hurricanes. Many have come our way to demonstrate their power. During the early fall months, names like Floyd, Ivan, Katrina, Irene, and Sandy dominated the front pages of newspapers, each killer event caused major heartache and grief.

And now a voice was telling me that there could be ways to lessen the power of these storms! I hoped *with all my heart* that what I was about to see was possible. How wonderful this would be.

It was at this point that a scene was forming in the huge window in front of me. Coming into view was a vast expanse of ocean with 10 large ships aligned in a row, all moving in one direction. They appeared different from any ocean-going craft ships I had seen before, and all were carrying some kind of huge machinery attached to their rear decks. I wondered what the function of this equipment had to do with hurricanes.

As if anticipating my curiosity, my guiding voice explained that cyclonic storms begin as tropical depressions and then build their strength from the heat of the warm waters that spawned them. The warmer, the better.

Often these depressions journey over vast stretches of warm water to allow their power to intensify into full hurricanes. However, when they pass over land, they tend to weaken temporarily, only to regain their strength as they again move over the open sea.

The voice then offered the following hypothesis: "What if the waters in the path of such storms were made substantially cooler so that they couldn't intensify?"

The voice continued, "Suppose there was a fleet of specially equipped super ice-producing machines capable of churning out tons of dry ice with a temperature of -109 degrees Fahrenheit as compared to the +32 degrees Fahrenheit of regular ice?"

"Suppose this ice could be continuously produced by massive systems mounted on the decks of these specially equipped boats?"

"Suppose the number of boats required could vary according to the potential path and growth of each storm?"

"Suppose these boats could be positioned directly at the initial point of formation of future hurricanes?"

What I was hearing and viewing in the window in front of me was fascinating. But the viability of the idea must be left for others to consider. Again, I am neither a meteorologist nor a scientist.

Nevertheless, the hypothesis of such methodology for taming hurricanes seems logical. To be sure, it appeared *doable* in my visions—and it still does!

But, its development will have to overcome a number of important hurdles. The first and most significant would be the funding for such a project. Governments throughout the world would have to agree on a method of sharing its costs. And that could require lots of debates and foot dragging.

What might the other remaining hurdles be? Determining the project's impact on the environment, the cruise and travel industry, the world's fishing industries, oceanographers' undersea explorations, and many other important interests that would insist their views be considered before any widespread approval could be granted. These were some of my concerns as this vision ended.

Frankly, the indelible image left in my mind was of that fleet of 10 dry ice-dispensing ships fading from view, almost like a television show drawing to a conclusion.

Even now, I wonder whether what I witnessed could eventually become the way hurricanes will be eliminated.

Who can say? After all, I am merely the messenger. But somehow I have a feeling everything I witness will eventually come to pass. The winds will be tamed. Coastal properties will no longer be endangered. People's lives will no longer be threatened.

Now you understand why I called this vision: CONTROLLING THE FORCE.

As was the case with all my other visions, I eventually found myself back where it had initially captured my attention, in this instance, in my Midwest hotel room. Once again, the clock indicated that no time had passed.

In case this is something I have failed to mention, in all of my visions, my clock, my watch, and any other device that tracks the time always indicate that I return within seconds of when I left on one of these unique interludes. How? I have spent many hours trying to come up with an answer, but in all honesty it would take an Einstein to offer a logical explanation.

Once back, however, I again began writing down everything I saw. Hopefully, my notes can eventually be turned into scientific-quality drawings. I am sure that if da Vinci had had such a vision, he could have turned what he saw into clear, highly accurate illustrations. This tends to reinforce my feeling that these different kinds of visions may have been the genesis of many of those richly depicted renderings he left to posterity.

Regardless, I wanted to make sure this "different" vision experience was included here, with all of the accounts of my normal visions that were continuing to occur with increasing regularity (as if any such happenings could ever be considered normal).

Not surprisingly, I soon found that my regular visions had not lost any of their potency.

VISION NO. 17

The Winds of War

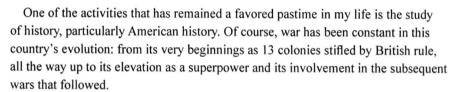

One of the activities that has remained a favored pastime in my life is the study of history, particularly American history. Of course, war has been constant in this country's evolution: from its very beginnings as 13 colonies stifled by British rule, all the way up to its elevation as a superpower and its involvement in the subsequent wars that followed.

Although war, big or small, is almost an inevitable and regrettable occurrence among nations, its aftermath provides an insightful way to understand the psychology of greed, ambition, and power. Too often, it is cultivated by secret groups to strengthen their power over areas rich in the commodities other nations crave—be it oil, precious metals, food, water, or huge populations of potential slave labor.

In some instances, these secret groups are not even government-affiliated, but rather, merely shadowy cabals aware that control over these key commodities creates power—the ultimate prize.

To accomplish this, they have to capture the minds of the peoples they control. This is often achieved by utilizing false issues of great national pride such as threats to their borders, existing hatred of neighboring countries, and most inflammatory of all, the utilization of violations of religious values.

Unfortunately, also too often, its fruits are delivered by the blood of men and women who go to their deaths for reasons *far different* from those they were led to believe.

That said, I want to underscore this fact: I abhor all killing.

It is sickening to consider the number of killed and wounded in our past encounters. The Civil War alone was America's bloodiest conflict: it resulted in nearly 1,100,000 casualties, among which were 620,000 deaths. Those lost constituted the heart of our nation's young people, desperately needed to help grow our burgeoning industries, railroads, cities, and farms. Instead, they were pawns for reasons that supported the interests of the powerful few, rather than the majority.

Consequently, we wound up with bodies strewn all across this young continent. Names like Chickamauga, Chancellorsville, Antietam, Shiloh, and Fredericksburg became battle cries for lesser-known battles. All the while, blood continued to spill and hatred between the North and South continued to grow; the battle of Gettysburg alone cost the Union 23,000 lives and the Confederacy 28,000.

The foreign wars that followed were equally cruel. World War I and World War II also produced stunning carnage. D-Day alone produced approximately 10,000 allied casualties and 15,000 among French civilians. Another 12,000 Americans died in Okinawa—and 19,000 died during the Battle of the Bulge.

I could go on by citing the staggering losses in Korea and Vietnam, but I hardly think it is necessary. War produces death in large numbers. But suppose such death could be preventable? What kind of debate might that possibly generate?

I raise this question because it was quite pertinent to my next incredible vision. Ironically, it came on Memorial Day.

I had arrived home after a series of appearances in different parts of the country. I was tired and ready for a restful evening of television. Tonight it was to be a program from Washington, D.C., commemorating the deaths of our service men and women who have fought in our many past and present conflicts.

Again, I should state up front that, despite the fact that I was fairly exhausted, I was still wide awake when the next vision embraced me and whisked me to some unknown time and place in the future.

I will describe everything that happened, beginning with my initial awareness that I was no longer was sitting in my favorite chair back home. In fact, I was now in a place that was far different.

I found myself standing on top of an expansive green hill. Ahead of me were large groups of people, some in civilian clothes, others in military uniforms. In the distance, I could hear the sound of explosions, while overhead I saw occasional jet fighters flying in formation. It was almost as if I was watching an action movie, but this was very real and rather overwhelming.

Still, I realized I was there in my usual spirit form, and of course, completely invisible and therefore able to move around freely. I looked down at the bottom of the hill, where there must have been at least a thousand soldiers in full battle gear, probably a whole battalion. Certainly an intimidating sight.

But what was such a large force doing there? My curiosity continued in high gear. I found myself wanting this information very badly.

On top of the hill, there was a small group of people seated in front of a platform containing a table, and it was obvious they were waiting for a briefing of some kind.

Being invisible, I did not hesitate to bring myself closer. I was hoping to read what was written on some documents which rested on the table's surface. Of course, in my current state, I could only look, but not touch.

What I saw were a pile of what appeared to be many folders. A few had some reports sticking out. One in particular caught my attention.

It had a date: April 14, 2020; at least I now knew what year I was in. Additionally, it displayed other information. Written boldly on its front page were the words: CLASSIFIED TEST. Directly below, the location of the test: CAMDEN, ARKANSAS (which I later determined was an independent ordnance testing facility).

This information only intensified my curiosity.

When I spotted a group of high-level military officers, I immediately moved closer. Fortunately, because of the noise from the distant explosions and the occasional flyovers, they had to raise their voices so they could hear each other. This, of course, made my eavesdropping easier.

Strangely, over and over, they kept using three words: "Mass Paralytic Intervention." A term that sounded important, intimidating and even scary, possibly some kind of new weapon.

In a matter of minutes, I was to learn that what these words referred to was hardly a weapon at all; in fact, far from it.

The explanation came from a colonel, now seated at the table with his companion officers. Using a microphone, he told us what we were about to observe. He explained that theoretically, they were two opposing groups of soldiers. The men directly below the hill were to be considered "Force D," or the defending contingents.

Approximately 500 yards beyond were an equal number of soldiers designated "Force A," the aggressors.

Each contingent was to wear colored armbands to distinguish them from each other, and to make them more visible from this position above.

So far, what he was describing seemed like just another typical exercise. I have seen many such "green army" vs. "blue army" kinds of maneuvers in the movies and on TV, but what was this one all about?

Frankly, I had no idea. Other than those three words: "Mass Paralytic Intervention." Not to mention, why were there so many apparently high-level VIPs in attendance?

Another of the military officers (this time a three-star general) took the small mic from the colonel's hand. I watched as he tapped on it two or three times to make sure his voice was properly amplified, and I realized this guy was probably the top man present. Hopefully, we would soon have the complete scoop.

This assumption was correct.

Specifically, he told us that we were about to witness the means to stop any advancing force "dead" in its tracks, and to render all participants incapable of any bodily movement whatsoever.

WHAT? The general's opening grabbed my attention. I noticed it also caught the attention of everyone else. They all began shouting questions.

They wanted to learn more. Lots more. He lifted his hand in a bid for silence, then the general launched into a long prologue detailing that what we were about to see and hear had taken years to develop, cost half a billion dollars and was for our eyes only.

With his opening comments completed, he pointed to several large wooden boxes that had just been unloaded from a military truck. As soon as the first one was opened, we could see it contained what appeared to be gas masks; not quite the old-fashioned kind, but nevertheless, masks obviously intended to protect all of us from something. We soon learned what that "something" was.

It was the Mass Paralytic Intervention, "MPI" (as he later called it), that he and his fellow officers had been talking about.

He went on to explain that it was the name of a breakthrough component developed by a secret contingent of United States government scientists working in conjunction with the Army Corps of Engineers. Together they had created a fluid which, when sprayed on advancing enemy troops, would put them in a totally immobile state, rendering them incapable of moving any part of their body for a full 10 minutes.

Amidst a combination of "oohs" and "ahhs" and a smattering of applause, he went on to explain that once the spray was deployed it would cover land areas up to half a mile, at which time our people wearing appropriate masks could close in, disarm the paralyzed enemy, and take them prisoner. No shots fired. No deaths.

He then requested everyone in attendance to put on one of the masks. Of course, in my current state, I found this unnecessary.

Interestingly, I could see that the soldiers in Force D directly below our vantage point also had been ordered to put their masks on.

The general then told us that upon a command given from this position, Force A, the aggressors, would be ordered to attack Force D, the defenders. He also indicated that both groups had been fully equipped with blank ammunition.

And then he gave the signal to start.

From our vantage point, we watched the panorama of simulated battle beginning to unfold below. We could hear the sound of machine gun and rifle fire from both groups. It was obvious the aggressors were getting close to the defenders, and it was at this point that three airplanes swept down and sprayed the attacking troops.

What followed was incredible.

Within minutes, gunfire ceased; every man appeared to be rigid, as if they were statues.

Then, exactly as the general indicated, the defending forces climbed out of their positions and moved forward to the silent forms in front of them. They disarmed them and placed white stickers on their uniforms, officially designating them as prisoners.

Almost as if to emphasize the importance of what we had just witnessed, the general placed a large clock containing a timing device on the table within everyone's view. He then set it in motion so that it would automatically count off 10 minutes.

We all watched as the hand repeatedly moved around the circumference of the clock until there was a ringing sound to indicate the 10 minutes were up.

Amazingly, as promised, the men below began to move. At this point, my mind was alive with questions. I wondered if all the people around me had the same ones.

Fortunately, the general was more than willing to reply to any query as long as the person asking the question identified him or herself. Here are some of the questions asked, complete with his answers (taken from my notes):

Question: Will the men below be 100% free of any permanent after-effects from what was sprayed on them?
Answer: Absolutely. They will not have even a headache or suffer any nausea.

Question: Isn't the use of gas outlawed under the Geneva Convention?
Answer: It is. But this technically is not a gas. It is a temporary agent that disarms nerve sensitivity for a very short period. Just long enough to render enemies helpless.

Question: Did the President sign off on this?
Answer: Yes.

Question: Did you in any manner get Congressional permission to use this weapon?
Answer: Let me correct you. This is not a weapon. It is an anti-weapon. In regard to Congressional permission, we did not go to Congress in the traditional sense; instead, we met in secret with several leading members of certain committees. They were plugged in all the way.

Question: Do you think this could eventually be a deterrent to war?
Answer: I hope so, but probably not. Keep in mind, this works only against people, not machines. So far, the only deterrents to machines are bombs and explosives. If we can knock out the people who control them, we might be knocking out the machines as well.

Question: Do you think this spray may eventually be used by police departments to replace bullets?

Answer: Let me make it clear, I may be a three-star general, but I deplore killing and guns. I would hope someday this material is not only distributed for police use, but made available to licensed civilian paramilitary companies.

There were more questions that were directed to the general, but I have chosen to share the most important ones. In fact, during the question and answer session, I felt myself fading away from the scene. Within seconds, I was actually back in my home watching the Memorial Day program on my television.

It was no surprise to me that the same speaker as before was still on camera, still concentrating on the same point as before I was transformed out of the room. As was always the case, no time had passed.

In thinking about what I had seen, my fondest hope, of course, is that the winds of a war never blow again. But if they ever do, may they be repelled by winds of our own. Winds that will contain this incredible spray that will instantly mute the strength of whoever dares to attack this great nation.

VISION NO. 18

A Towering Vision

I have always been fascinated by heights. This probably makes sense, considering how much time I actually spend flying each year. In fact, I am often kidded by friends and family who ask me if I intend to exchange my frequent flyer miles for a controlling interest in an airline company.

Not likely. However, often when I am soaring above ground at an altitude of 30,000-plus feet, I marvel at all the people who make their living working at extraordinary heights. These brave individuals not only include pilots, astronauts, and the "hard hat" workers who build the world's skyscrapers, dams and electronic towers—but also certain entertainers, particularly, tightrope walkers. Yes, I said tightrope walkers.

I have great respect for them given all of the risks they take. As a performer, I am well aware of the need to keep an audience enthralled. I also know the fear of making a mistake up there on stage; if I slip up, it could result in great embarrassment. But if they slip up—it could result in death.

Yet, over the past century, thousands of these brave individuals have continued to risk their lives to entertain cheering crowds, most under the big top, amidst the atmosphere of pomp and pageantry only a circus can create.

Still, there are certain other tightrope walkers who willingly take their thrills outdoors, tackling the kinds of impossible challenges many would consider insane to attempt.

But often, the more insane a challenge, the more appealing it has been to members of the Wallenda family, the world's most renowned aerialists – a group I appeared with in Canada. But be assured, I did not walk any tightropes.

A case in point: on June 15, 2012, America held its breath as Nik Wallenda mounted a stretch of wire spanning an 1,800-foot portion of Niagara Falls. He was well aware of the many millions of viewers watching his attempt on the ABC TV network to traverse the treacherous distance in front of him. He also realized there were some hoping for an even greater thrill—to witness him falling to his death.

Nevertheless, he not only set forth on his dangerous journey, but he accomplished his mission with great skill and showmanship. I was among those in the television audience that day, and I, too, was fascinated with the events unfolding on the screen.

As a performer, I wondered what thoughts might have been occupying his mind as he made his way across the roaring water below him. Fear? Possibly. Determination? Absolutely. But perhaps there was something else.

Could he have been thinking about his great-grandfather, Karl Wallenda, who was killed in a fall in 1978 while attempting to cross a lesser distance connecting two hotel towers in Puerto Rico?

Yes, that stark recollection might have been dancing in his mind, but Nik kept moving forward, step by step, until he accomplished his goal. To me, Nik Wallenda personifies everything that is admirable about tightrope walkers. What also earns my admiration is that they keep doing the things they do, usually for no better reason than that these incredible feats have yet to be successfully achieved. However, considering risk against reward, few tightrope walkers have ever died rich.

But there is another reason I have focused on these under appreciated performers: they played an important part of my next vision.

(NOTE: I want to once more reiterate that for the most part I have no idea why I am ever drawn into the kinds of visions described in this book. It is easy to conclude that they may be due to something I have seen, heard, or discussed. But rarely could I make a solid case for what that "something" might be. That is—up to now.)

Let me explain. I had just completed an engagement in San Francisco. I usually occupy an aisle seat on long-distance flights so that I can get up and walk occasionally without disturbing anyone near me. Still, I often wish I could peer down below when flying over any area that has particular sights of great beauty: the Grand Canyon is one such spot, another is the skyline of New York City. And still another, my beloved Las Vegas—daytime or evening.

But it is consistently San Francisco that appeals to me the most. It has always been my opinion that Tony Bennett nailed it in describing his love affair for The City by the Bay. Perhaps this last flyover was what triggered my next vision.

The trip back from California to the east coast had been long and bumpy. As usual, it was good to be back home; I was hungry and rustled up some makings for a sandwich and flipped on the television.

The screen soon filled with an old movie, *Trapeze*. A brief synopsis described it as focusing on the emotions and skills of daring aerialists. I mention this only as a possible clue as to what was to follow.

I had neither taken a bite of my sandwich, nor settled into total relaxation mode when this next vision took over. I was immediately whisked to another far-off location. (Yes, that is how they happen: no warning, no factoring my fatigue or readiness) This "trip" required no more than a blink of an eye, but once there, I could not believe where I had just been taken.

I remember thinking, "What? Again?" I was actually back in San Francisco, but this time at a great vantage point: I was standing in what appeared to be a temporary grandstand. This one was rather large and overlooking the Golden Gate Bridge. Yes, a trip that had recently taken more than five hours by plane to return home, required less than a second by the mysterious forces that create these visions to bring me back.

But why?

There appeared to be people standing on each of the towers of the bridge. Bells immediately went off in my mind. Was some fool going to attempt to traverse the 4,200 feet between each of these edifices? I soon realized the answer was a profound YES.

The day was clear. Looking around, I could see super-large television screens mounted in key spots. There was also a platform in front of these stands, containing the usual chairs and tables. All around me, people were beginning to take their seats in the grandstand.

After approximately 30 minutes, an ON THE AIR sign lit up and the master of ceremonies for this event appeared on the screens. He was soon followed by a split-screen picture of two small groups of people in the Golden Gate towers. One group was seemingly assigned to assist in the initiation of the walk, the other to handle the final steps of its completion.

At that point, I looked at the bridge itself. Its almost-one-mile-long length was impressive, but on the TV monitor it looked even longer. The split screen then focused on what appeared to be a long wire similar to what I had witnessed in the walk across Niagara Falls.

As was my usual first reaction, I wanted to know the date. I already knew where I was. Being invisible, I could of course wander about freely in hopes of obtaining some additional information—which is exactly what I did.

It required mere minutes to spot someone reading his morning newspaper containing exactly what I wanted to know.

On its front page in two-inch type was the date: September 9, 2025. Beneath it, the headline, "Celebrating California's 175th Anniversary, Tower-to-Tower High Wire Golden Gate Bridge Walk."

Now, here is the strange part: for whatever reason, I was not allowed to envision the name of the person making this incredible attempt. I had no doubt this was deliberate, and it raised all sorts of questions as to why. It did not take much time before I had my answer.

The master of ceremonies announced that the walker (whose identity continued to be hidden from me) was about to step onto the wire. It was a tense moment.

I watched, as did probably millions of people everywhere. I realized that in addition to conquering the great distance involved, this individual also had to somehow compensate for the winds swirling above and beneath the bridge. To say they could be very unpredictable over San Francisco Bay would probably be a gross understatement.

However, a late announcement informed viewers his wire had been drawn as tight as possible to provide firmer footing and to reduce the sway factor. In addition, we were told he was using some kind of scientifically developed pole containing shifting weights to aid his balance. Nevertheless, I kept thinking it probably would have been a better idea to provide him with a parachute.

Below, in the Bay, were numerous police and other emergency vessels. Everything inside of me kept telling me this was a crazy venture. I only wish I knew the identity of this brave, courageous, possibly insane individual, but whenever his name was mentioned, for some mysterious reason, it was not being made known to me.

Meanwhile, he had mounted the wire and had proceeded about one quarter of the distance to his destination. From what I could determine, he appeared calm and in total control. Then suddenly, he started to lean slightly to his right, almost as if he was about to fall. Those around me gasped, but he immediately regained both his balance and his composure and continued his incredible journey.

From that point on, as he took each step on that amazing quest, my admiration grew. This was indeed a tightrope walker like no other. Courageous? Certainly. Slightly out of his mind? Possibly. But above all else, he had great skill and determination in addressing his goal.

I now had suspicions as to who this daring individual was.

Approximately two hours later, he took the final step in achieving his goal. Amidst roars from the crowd, he confidently stepped off the wire and onto the tower platform. The crowd had to be held back from rushing the bridge. Fireworks were now filling the sky. I was shaking my head in disbelief. He had succeeded, and I had been wrong in estimating his chances.

In retrospect, if my suspicions as to who this person was had been verified in advance, my estimation of his chances of succeeding would have been different.

I will not speculate here who I think it was because if it was meant for me to be aware of his identity, it would have been made known in the vision. I only hope I am around in the year 2025 to not only again witness this spectacular feat, but also to confirm my suspicions as to who achieved this incredible accomplishment.

It was at this point, with the sounds of all those cheers still resonating in my head, that I suddenly found myself whisked back to my home in New Jersey. As I looked around my bedroom, I had to take a few minutes to literally catch my breath. I felt as if I had almost shared the walk behind him.

It was an adventure I will never forget. But this again led me to question the purpose of my being part of all these visions in the first place—particularly this one.

Was it to make a statement that whatever seems impossible today may become suddenly possible tomorrow? Or was it a lesson in personal humility, that even The Amazing Kreskin, with all his power of judgment and mental prowess, can be wrong? Particularly in judging the determination of any human being in overcoming impossible odds? Perhaps.

VISION NO. 19

Gun Control That Works

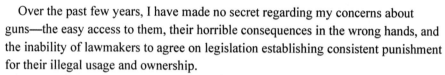

Over the past few years, I have made no secret regarding my concerns about guns—the easy access to them, their horrible consequences in the wrong hands, and the inability of lawmakers to agree on legislation establishing consistent punishment for their illegal usage and ownership.

I do believe in the Second Amendment, the right to keep and bear arms. However, what I do not agree with is the interpretation by some as to the exact definition of the blanket term "arms." Technically, this could mean tanks, mortars, machine guns, hand grenades, and on and on. Sound crazy? Not to those who put their own spin on the Second Amendment.

I am mindful that the United States of America was born out of a revolution fought by farmers, merchants, bankers, tavern owners, and people of all stripes and means who used whatever weapons they could muster to win independence for this nation.

For the most part, these weapons consisted of muskets and flintlocks and whatever other arms could be captured from the British. Certainly none of the participants in this uprising owned anything comparable to the kinds of high-powered assault devices being legally purchased under today's gun laws.

This is a hot issue currently being argued by various interests, not the least of which are the manufacturers and importers of these new classes of firearms, very few of which were truly designed to meet the needs of hunters or average citizens seeking protection for their homes and families. Current laws allow for their ownership when they are appropriately licensed and certain criteria is met.

But such licensing often is not enough to ensure the general public's safety, because of the easy accessibility of such weapons to those suffering from psychological disorders, and to those who would use them as seen on television, in action movies, or throughout video games.

Surprisingly, there is no age limit on these potential users. They range from the elderly all the way down to young children. And unfortunately, these weapons are often too easily accessed, either by family members from a gun rack left carelessly unlocked or from a law officer's holster slung over the back of a chair.

To make matters worse, there are a great many "other" guns: the forbidden kind. Too many are smuggled across state and international borders and peddled to mobsters, members of street gangs, and petty thieves. These dealers haul in huge profits.

Why is this so easy?

Because these weapons are usually sanitized, their serial numbers filed off to hide what is often an infamous and bloody trail. This makes them nearly impossible to trace when used in the commission of everything from robberies and assaults to murder for hire.

For the longest time now, I have hoped there would be some kind of creative legislation passed to enable the ferreting out and prosecution of people suspected of hiding illegal, unlicensed guns. Sadly, I am constantly reminded that such extraordinary measures could possibly violate a myriad of current laws.

I can reveal some startling good news.

There is a reason I titled this vision GUN CONTROL THAT WORKS. It was the result of a recent mystical excursion that allowed me to peer ahead to a whole new solution to this very sensitive issue. A method totally dependent upon technology— which is admittedly not yet on the current horizon, but, unless I am very much mistaken, *will be* the future. This vision was another of the kind in which I was simply a spectator.

I remind you, this is an experience where I was not taken to any event or happening. It was obvious I was only transitioned to watch, listen and, hopefully, learn.

This mysterious excursion took me from a dressing room in a Midwestern theater to that same small area I had been transported to during my "hurricane control" vision. I was hardly surprised that nothing within its four walls had changed. It contained the same simple wooden chair and a huge window.

As was the case during my first visit to this tiny confine, I found myself focused on the window. I knew it would soon contain my newest vision and I wasn't disappointed.

In this instance, I was to observe a scientist, white coat and all, standing by a chart containing a large diagram of what appeared to be a firearm of some kind.

(NOTE: What follows are my observations taken from my notes. This experience began exactly as my first "spectator" encounter did, with a male voice calmly indicating that all that I was about to see would be explained.)

In the scientist's hand was a long pointer, which he used to draw attention to a black circle prominently featured in a box appearing on the diagram. "This," he said, "is a microdot. It is precisely the size of the head of a pin. It is expected it will greatly diminish the threat of death or assault due to the use of unlawful weapons."

With those words, a sudden rush of excitement locked-in every essence of my attention.

I had no idea exactly what I was looking at, but within minutes its function became imminently clear. The scientist went on to describe it as having the capability of sending out a non-stop signal within a radius of 1,000 feet from any place in which it was attached.

He then provided me with the following information (which I have placed in the order it was provided):

1. He and fellow scientists had mastered a way of attaching this constantly transmitting microdot to any gun manufactured for private citizen use.

2. Supreme Court approval was granted for such attachment (using the same basis for legality as for the monitoring devices attached to automobiles to trace them in case of theft) as of the beginning of the coming year (which, according to the voice, was 2019).

3. Names and addresses of owners would be downloaded into the information banks of all police cars. This information would give them the ability to match their data with the signals emitted from all such weapons containing microdot attachments.

4. Should any police car containing such monitoring capability pass any structure from which a signal was being emitted where there was no owner indicated in their downloaded records, the technology would allow the police to investigate the source of the signal and make appropriate inquiries.

5. The pinpoint accuracy of the monitoring device would be similar to that used to trace minute fragments of satellites and meteors that had broken apart in space.

6. There would be no "grandfather" clause pertaining to legally licensed guns. Owners of such weapons would be given 90 days to take them to designated branding centers, where the microdots could be implanted over a 24-hour period.

These were the key points made clear by the voice as I watched and listened, fascinated and exhilarated by what had been made known to me. I very much wanted to hear more, but the picture soon faded and the voice turned to a whisper.

In a matter of seconds, it all ended. I found myself back in my dressing room. I sat there, stunned and exhilarated by what I had just experienced.

My fondest hope is that, among all of the many important revelations I have received over the past five years, this one in particular will turn into reality.

VISION No. 20

Target: Earth

The visions I have experienced during the past five years have convinced me that we live in extremely dangerous times. This feeling is reinforced by what is best described as an inward need to constantly maintain my mind in a vigilant mode.

Nevertheless, I still feel our nation is a place bolstered by a strong sense of character and decency. Almost too decent. So much so that I keep wondering when all of this might be threatened.

Will some horrific vision come to me at any moment foretelling that all we value, all that we cherish, could be in imminent jeopardy?

Strangely, it came to me upon my return from a well-received appearance in Florida. I was feeling almost euphoric. My show had gone extremely well, and the audience was highly receptive. They had come to see me perform "miracles" of the mind (including the finding of my hidden pay check, which went over in its usual impressive manner). Everything had transpired marvelously. To make matters even more satisfying, my flight home to New Jersey was smooth and uneventful.

That is why, when I later sat back to enjoy a few hours of relaxation, I had every reason to believe this would be as pleasant and peaceful an evening as anyone could hope for. But as events turned out, it was not.

In fact, it was as far from peaceful as I could possibly imagine.

I was about to pour myself a small glass of wine when that familiar feeling of the onset of a vision started to return. I wish I could put into words exactly what the sensation is like, all I can say is that it is different from anything you might imagine. Not painful, just incredibly different. That is why, once it begins, my usual reaction is not to resist, but simply go with the flow.

However, this time I wish I had fought back. Why?

Because this "flow" was about to take me to an event that might make the pages of scientific journals and more significantly, those of history books.

In mere seconds, I found myself in as frightening a setting as any I had ever seen. My first reaction was that I had been cast into the bowels of hell.

(NOTE: Once again, what follows was re-created from notes that I made immediately upon my return from these disturbing happenings.)

My first reaction was horror.

All around me, there were cries for help, buildings on fire, fallen walls, pipes gushing huge streams of water, sounds of sirens, and chaos unlike anything I had previously experienced. It was obvious something terrible had happened. But what?

Fortunately, in my spirit-like condition, I was immune to pain or physical danger.

Not so for the people cowering on the ground. Some appeared to be in a state of shock; others were hysterical, confused, and terrified. My mind was on high alert. I had to determine what had caused all of this.

I walked aimlessly through what seemed to be the main street of a city.

Cars were strewn about like toy blocks. Crackling wires and recurring distant explosions formed a background chorus of ominous sounds.

After about a mile, I came across a clearing.

Nearby, three helicopters were standing with their rotors still turning. I could also see several military trailers grouped together to form a sort of complex. Judging by the guards and the cables connected to numerous portable generators, this appeared to be a makeshift center for emergency operations.

I spent a few minutes observing people going in and out of the complex. However, my curiosity soon got the best of me. So, being invisible, I simply followed the next group that entered.

Inside was like another world. It was crowded with military and civilian authorities, flown in from who knows where. Many were talking on cell phones. Some were deeply involved in strategic discussions. Still others were monitoring computers and numerous other electronic devices.

The prevailing feeling of tension and fear was unmistakable. Making matters worse was the subdued lighting and eerie colors flashing from screens alive with graphics of mostly maps and charts.

I leaned closer to possibly determine what was being revealed on the monitors. It took a little time, but I eventually concluded they were intermittently displaying several satellite images of areas somewhere between Russia and China, and many of areas in Mongolia. However, language difficulties enabled me to determine only the year, which was 2019.

Furthermore, very little English was being spoken, which made it difficult to eavesdrop on the various conversations taking place all around me. Nevertheless, it was obvious something ominous was happening.

Detecting some words of English from the far other side of the complex, I made my way there and located a group that seemingly spoke my language. I assumed they were staff members of either western embassies or of international news services. I hoped they were fluent enough to provide accurate and timely information as to what was going on.

I was not to be disappointed. (NOTE: I almost wish I was.)

Specifically, they were confirming preliminary reports that the cause of all the destruction and chaos was the possible explosion of an asteroid approximately 60 miles from the capital city of Mongolia, above the city of Ulan Bator, which had a population of more than one million people.

While the force of the blast and the resulting fragments had caused substantial damage to many outlying structures as it skimmed over the earth's surface, it had actually missed the city entirely. Nevertheless, its reverberations resulted in many civilian injuries and considerable loss of life.

My mind immediately flashed to another relatively recent asteroid explosion that had occurred over Russia.

It happened on February 15, 2013. The asteroid had burst over the city of Chelyabinsk after soaring across the sky at 40,000 miles per hour. The resulting damage was felt as far away as 50 miles. It was deemed one of the worst catastrophes in modern-day history. In fact, over 1,500 people had been injured and thousands of buildings destroyed.

Scientists later confirmed its explosion was equivalent to that of 400,000 tons of TNT and produced a burst of light 30 times brighter than the sun.

There had also been an earlier asteroid explosion over Russia. This one was over Tunguska, Siberia, in 1908. There still exists substantial controversy whether the resulting destruction was actually due to the presence of an asteroid, or whether it was something else.

Some investigators believed the damage might have been caused by some other mysterious force, possibly even atomic in nature. However, in 1908, there was no such thing as atomic power, at least not on this planet. This prompted some conspiracy theorists to raise doubts as to the date the explosion actually occurred. Some believed it had possibly happened centuries earlier.

What immediately concerned me was getting a closer look at this current catastrophe. I had no way of knowing whether I was now actually somewhere in Mongolia, however, judging by what was going on around me, I had to assume I was. If so, I had to get to a view close to the point of impact. My next question was, how?

None of the helicopters seemed to be taking off so I had to find an alternative method of transportation. Fortunately, this problem was soon resolved. On the debris- littered avenue in front of the tents and trailers, there was a steady stream of military vehicles all heading in one direction, which I concluded was toward the closest area of impact. I simply climbed on board and went along for the ride.

As I looked around, it was not too surprising to find its occupants wearing special suits to protect them from radiation or any other negative emanations from whatever might have visited us from outer space. Of course, I had no need for such a garment.

The journey to our destination lasted approximately four hours and was hampered by the recurrent need to go off road to avoid fallen trees and rocks of all sizes. But once we arrived, I realized those on board were wise to wear the protective garments, because I was soon staring at what appeared to be a huge piece of an asteroid. To the naked eye, it looked like an ordinary rock, only this one was probably millions of years old.

There were many observers hovering around its circumference. However, the dangers it posed were obvious. I could hear the unmistakable sounds of instruments constantly alive with the crackling of radioactivity. At the same time, cameras were capturing every angle of the object. I had little doubt these images were being transmitted to laboratories and crisis centers all over the world.

Obviously, what I was looking at was not the whole asteroid. From the occasional comments in English, it was apparent this was but a fragment blown apart from the original, but still, it was approximately 40 feet in circumference.

As pieces of its surface were being carefully chipped off to send back to laboratories, I wondered how big the actual asteroid had been. I also noted that because the area was alive with radioactivity, it was being cordoned off to keep unauthorized personnel at a safe distance.

Meanwhile, I moved among those who were permitted within the perimeter. I still wanted to know what they now knew. Fortunately, I again found some people talking in English.

From their conversation, I was able to determine that the object was indeed an asteroid; estimates had it exploding approximately 15 miles above the Earth. Fragments such as the one being examined in front of me had reportedly been strewn over a wide swath of unpopulated area.

Based on the examination of this large fragment and others found at different sites, the whole asteroid was believed to be no fewer than 70 feet in diameter before bursting. If so, this would make it larger than the one that broke apart above Chelyabinsk.

At that point, it appeared nearly impossible to determine the immediate and long-term effects on Ulan Bator and other cities in Mongolia that suffered significant death and damage. From what I could determine, the fallout was massive and widespread. I had little doubt that this event would occupy a very prominent place in the history books along with those that had exploded over Russia.

My only hope is that by the year 2019 there will be some means to engage with such objects, either to shatter them well before their arrival near our planet, or somehow alter their path. I will leave this for our future's scientists to ponder.

Later, back in my room, as I had done countless times before, I wondered why these visions are made known to me. Even though many of these glimpses into the future tell of positive happenings, discoveries, inventions and ways to make life better, this one did not.

I still ponder whether there will be other such objects, possibly many times larger bearing down on any of the world's most populated cities. God forbid such an occurrence ever happens. Nevertheless, I will stay on the alert.

VISION No. 21

The Winter's Tale

—————⌘—————

Much of my professional life is dependent on getting to where I have to be. For the most part, that means the roads must be clear and the airlines free of delays. The year 2014 played havoc with my schedule; the chief culprits were snow, ice and cold, so much so that it seemed to never want to end.

In fact, southern states that rarely face many of winter's horrors were hit multiple times. Of course, the Northeast quadrant of the U.S. not only saw significant numbers of these massive wintery blasts, but well beyond anyone's expectations, even my own. Records were broken, lines were down, and shelters were packed.

This unyielding repetition of storms had weather forecasters calling this consistent cold, ice and snow a new kind of super "Polar Vortex."

Among the questions I am asked repeatedly (both on stage and off) pertain to the weather. My usual answer: "To be of real assistance, I would have to be connected to the Great Weather Maker Upstairs. In truth, I depend on the same forecasters as everyone else does."

That pretty much sums it up. As perceptive as my mental resources are, they do not provide advance weather reports. I would probably be better off relying on some of the joints in my body to forecast future meteorological conditions. At least, that's what I thought.

In early February I was in an Atlanta, Georgia motel. My return flight back to Newark had been cancelled, which meant the possibility of not making scheduled appearances in the Northeast tri-state area. I mentally accepted my situation and tried to do the next best thing -- relax. But that was not to be, because once again, it was vision time.

Suddenly, I found myself standing in the middle of Times Square. Yes, the crossroads of the world, only not this particular day: all around me was an unbelievable panorama of white: hills of snow absolutely impassable to pedestrians or cars.

Furthermore, none of the area's iconic advertising signs or lights were visible; except for one, the illuminated news ribbon winding around the old *New York Times* building. Somehow, it was working. In retrospect, this access to the news probably explains why I had been transported to this particular spot: merely looking up, I could get some idea as to what was happening and when.

I almost wished I had not seen it, because the explanation was incredible.

New York City and its five boroughs were being pummeled by a mid-January 51-inch snowfall. The year indicated on the feed was 2020 (yes, I had been transported six years into the future). The city's surrounding areas—Long Island, New Jersey and Connecticut—had also been hit hard. Their projected total: 60 inches plus. To make matters worse, the current temperature was minus 3 degrees Fahrenheit.

In my lifetime, I had never expected a mid-Northeast United States winter assault like this one; perhaps in Maine or New Hampshire, but never in New York City.

Still, as stark and frightening as this scene was, it appeared almost pristine. Unfortunately, it also indicated numerous potential dangers: impassable roads, people suffering from loss of power, the inability to obtain emergency medical attention, an immobilized police force, and fire departments unable to respond. Despite its stark beauty, it was also a horror.

The continuous *New York Times* feed overhead provided further details. The storm had hit the previous Friday night; it was now Sunday, which theoretically would have given the city the opportunity to mobilize its resources to attempt to dig out. But the effectiveness of that endeavor was in question: additional snow was forecast beginning that evening and expected to continue into the next morning.

To make matters worse, drivers were being told to stay off the roads, airports had cancelled all flights, and schools and businesses were closed. Attempts were being made to open neighborhood shelters, and wherever possible, hospital personnel were requested to somehow report for duty. I remember thinking to myself, "How were they to get there? By dog sled?"

By now I could hear the sound of heavy-duty trucks several blocks away. There appeared to be 20 or so large sanitation vehicles equipped with front-mounted snowplows, attempting to carve some kind of pathway through the area intersecting Broadway with 7th Avenue.

First impression: impossible. After all, they were attacking accumulations over four feet deep. But these New York snow removal folks are a tough and experienced breed, so I had little doubt they would accomplish their mission.

I now wanted to observe other areas. So I began wandering through the middle of Times Square. In my spirit state, this was not too difficult. I was weightless. However, I could easily see that for any normal person, trudging through 60 inches of snow would be nearly impossible.

My goal was to try and reach the far west side of Manhattan because I wanted to observe the condition of the Hudson River. I realized to make that possible I would have to jump aboard anything moving in my desired direction. As you might imagine, it turned out to be a snowplow, in a line directly behind other plows, so we managed to creep along, not fast, but continuously.

As we headed across town, there were signs hanging from windows asking for help. Not just asking, but many begging. Some had the word EMERGENCY written in red. Others said: NO HEAT or NO FUEL. Others asked for an ambulance. I could only surmise that 911 lines were jammed as never before. My sympathies went out to these poor individuals who were probably hungry, cold, frightened, and in desperate need of assistance.

But all I could do was observe. Finally, I could see the Hudson River; the trip had taken approximately 30 minutes.

This huge waterway is impressive. It flows adjacent to New York's crucial West Side Highway, all the way up to the state's capital in Albany. This important north-to-south road is where we stopped.

By now, I had left the truck and ventured towards the water's edge. To my surprise (I might even say, my utter shock), there were people walking on the river's ice-covered surface.

My next reaction was that if they felt safe doing it, why shouldn't I? Particularly in my weightless state; after all, what could happen? So I did what I never in my whole life expected to do: walk on water, and on the Hudson River, no less.

Being invisible, I approached the individuals on the iced surface. They wore identification tags indicating they were weather reporters from some local TV station. I watched as they drilled a hole in the ice to measure its depth. The answer: seven inches.

I remembered when in studying New York history, that the city had experienced some awful winter events in the 18th and 19th centuries. For instance, the Hudson had previously frozen in 1720, 1734, 1780, and many other times in the 19th century. On the other side of Manhattan, the East River had frozen in 1813, 1817, 1821, 1851, 1857, 1867, and 1875. In fact, the resulting ice was solid enough to function as the perfect pedestrian bridge to Brooklyn and what is now Queens.

Crossing the river in this manner became so popular, that for a few coins, young boys would provide ladders at certain spots along the banks of the river on both sides so that people could safely climb to and from the water's edge. However, there were several incidents in which people fell through cracks in the ice.

One such incident involved steamboat inventor Robert Fulton attempting to rescue a friend who slipped through an opening in the ice one night upon returning from a party. Fulton tried desperately to save him, but to no avail. As a result of his becoming soaking wet, he developed pneumonia, which, along with other lung problems, eventually led to his early death from tuberculosis in 1815 at age 49. By 1867, the number of these accidents helped stimulate the demand for a real Brooklyn Bridge.

This mysterious vision of an incredible winter in the year 2020 ended as suddenly as it began. One moment, I was standing on the icy surface of the Hudson, and the next I was back in my warm Atlanta hotel room. I can only assume this vision of what might hit the Northeast quadrant of the United States in the year 2020 was given to me as a warning for the cities and towns in the area to be prepared. However, deep down, I hope this never comes to pass.

VISION No. 22

A New Perspective On How Animals Evolve

Over the past five years, I have ceased being surprised where my visions take me. I have become used to seeing burning buildings, floods, incredible medical discoveries, daring stunts, and people of power doing incredible things, but this next vision was far different from anything I had previously experienced.

In truth, it was actually a fun happening. So much so, it made me look forward to the year 2019. You will understand why further along.

As usual, it occurred at a time when I least wanted the "spirit me" transported to some other place: a mere few seconds before I was due on stage for a rescheduled show in eastern Long Island.

Even though I have been doing what I do for over 50 years, I still get tense standing in the wings awaiting an introduction; it is then that my mind is fully focused on my opening comments to an audience that has paid the ultimate compliment by purchasing tickets to a Kreskin performance.

Nevertheless, when the "powers that be" choose to take over, they are in full command. Once again, I was catapulted to a whole new place to view events occurring at a whole new time.

Ironically, the last thing I saw before being whisked away was a backstage sign saying NO PETS ALLOWED. As events developed, I later wondered if this was some kind of fate-generated joke.

As to the vision itself, transportation took but a flash, a mere blink. Followed by my usual question: Where was I?

In this instance, the answer did not require too much thought. I sensed right away the kind of facility in which I had been deposited; it was a large auditorium, probably a wing of a college or university building. The venue had that kind of "imposing" feeling, possibly because it could, and did, accommodate over 1,500 people.

Furthermore, it appeared all its seats were filled. But they were not there to see a Kreskin demonstration.

Not this time. I could tell this was something far different. That is why my immediate priority was to determine what the attraction was. I also wanted to obtain a better view of who was occupying the seats. Fortunately, in my invisible state, this was hardly a problem.

As I walked down the aisles, my guess was that many appeared to be academics, along with their whole families (kids and all) and, surprisingly, members of the media. Their presence was obvious because of the ID worn around their necks and numerous television cameras (and their crews) ready to communicate whatever was about to take place.

But what might that be? And why would children be present? Then I heard strange sounds.

There were many of them. Almost like a discordant blend of screeching, howling and roaring, all morphing into a bellowing chorus with few of the sounds being exactly the same.

Some were loud. Some were soft. I was not sure of who or what might be producing them. They provided the only clue as to what this special event might be.

Then the answer fell in place. Of course!

Yes, animals, here, in some type of school auditorium.

I seemed to be the only one who was able to hear them, which was not surprising. My extrasensory skills provided an enhanced level of hearing, which is customary when I am in the midst of one of these sudden "vision" experiences.

My first reaction was that this was some kind of indoor circus. The wide stage certainly appeared conducive to such a performance. So what kind of vision was I about to witness? And why?

Fortunately, the suspense did not last long. Suddenly, the loudspeakers were transmitting the theme song from the Dr. Doolittle film, "If I Could Talk to the Animals."

I now wondered if what was about to take place were demonstrations of attempted communication with wild beasts. However, what actually ensued far exceeded anything referred to in the lyrics of the song.

While all eyes were focused on the stage, walking down the aisle came a man dressed in the garb of an animal trainer, a bright red costume with gold-trimmed epaulets. But it was what he had on a leash walking beside him that caused many in the audience to gasp: a huge Bengal tiger, a cat that looked as ferocious as it was handsome.

To make matters more frightening, the animal was letting out intermittent roars; this time, the kind EVERYONE could hear. Nevertheless, the audience seemed appropriately confident that the heavy, chained leash was sufficient to restrain the beast. At least, that's what they thought at first.

What happened next changed a lot of minds.

The huge cat gave an unexpected lunge that was strong enough for the trainer to suddenly drop the chain.

The tiger was free.

Screams for help could be heard everywhere. Panic was about to take hold. I recall it becoming obvious that unless some kind of intervention took place immediately, the audience would bolt for the exits.

Fortunately, the needed intervention did appear. A small army of security guards circled the animal while a voice on the loudspeaker urged everyone to stay calm and reassured them with the surprising announcement that what they had seen was all part of the show.

I kept thinking "All part of the show?!"

Had its planners given this any real thought? If anyone had been trampled, the results would have been tragic. What kind of bizarre presentation was this?

Meanwhile, the trainer simply called out a command.

Upon hearing his voice, the animal stopped and slowly returned to where the leash had fallen. Amazingly, the tiger just lay down and waited while the chain was reattached. He then allowed himself to be marched onto the huge stage and back to his cage, which remained open.

Having been told that the animal's escape was all part of the show, I now could hardly wait to see whether the real show would surpass what I had already witnessed.

Indeed, it would.

There was a drum roll, and the curtains lifted to reveal a huge backstage area. It had to be massive, because it was now filled with many colorful cages of all sizes and shapes, the largest of which was occupied by two of nature's fiercest denizens: a lion and what appeared to be at least a nine-foot grizzly bear. In stark contrast, close by, there stood a giant glass aviary with many small birds fluttering about.

It was at that moment that I recall a banner being lowered across the full length of the stage that made it clear what all of these people had come to see. It read, DR. ARNO'S 2019 EXHIBITION OF FIERCE ANIMALS TAMED BEYOND IMAGINATION.

Hard to believe this is what had attracted this large audience. Why had I been transported years into the future to view an indoor circus that really was a glorified animal act? What made it special? I was soon to find out.

A master of ceremonies of sorts then introduced the trainer as an internationally famous handler of animals of all species and sizes. As indicated by the banner, his name was Dr. Anthony Arno.

After some polite applause, Arno proceeded to the cage that held the bear and the lion and opened the door. This time, instead of bolting off wildly, these large beasts simply exited the cage and sat on the floor close to the trainer.

I almost couldn't believe what I was seeing: here were two of the world's most incompatible animals sitting calmly side by side.

What happened next added significantly to the excitement of what had already been demonstrated. Without saying a word, Arno excused himself and walked to the wings. The curious audience, sensitive to any new surprises, seemed apprehensive as to what might now take place. They soon breathed easier, because in a matter of minutes he returned in the midst of a bright spotlight, now accompanied by a lad whom he introduced as his son, Arlo.

I chuckled to myself, noting the youngster's first and last name: Arlo Arno. The audience seemed to enjoy it, as well. Nevertheless, it had no visible effect on the boy, who seemed to be no older than 9 or 10. In fact, he displayed but one emotion: pride; possibly because he was costumed in an outfit that was an exact duplicate of his father's.

By now, Dr. Arno was prodding the lion with a thin whip-like cane he was carrying. The restless beast responded with several roars and showed its displeasure by raising a paw in a gesture of defiance. It seemed to me that the King of the Jungle was beginning to display signs of annoyance. It was as if this was what Arno had been waiting for.

Without any hesitation, he requested that his son remove his hat, then, to the amazement of all, led him by the hand closer to the lion's huge head. The bear, meanwhile, was also now voicing his aroused anger.

It was at that point that I began to wonder, was Arno going to risk doing the unthinkable? As it turned out, my apprehension was right on the mark.

The crowd, also sensing what was about to happen, began to shout out their concerns. Some were even yelling for the police.

Without a word to an audience that had suddenly grown hostile, Arno boldly parted the lion's jaws and instructed his son to put his small head inside the lion's mouth.

Amidst cries from every part of the auditorium to STOP, the lad immediately obeyed his father's order.

To the horror of everyone watching, the youngster placed his head inside the animal's huge mouth and proceeded to keep it there for a full 10 seconds before allowing his father to pull it out. The audience kept screaming. By now, some were even shaking their fists.

However, neither boy nor lion seemed any the worse for what had just transpired. Still, it seemed Arno felt the lion had not completely demonstrated his willingness to comply.

Without any hesitation, Dr. Arno pointed to a large electric timer hanging where it could be seen by everyone in the audience. The master of ceremonies made it known that, upon Arno's signal, it would be set to ring in exactly 25 seconds.

Arno then personally opened the animal's mouth wide, this time placing his own head in its cavernous depths. I remember thinking there probably were those in the audience hoping the beast would clamp down on it immediately. But even though the huge animal was again raising one of its paws in protest, I could see that the doctor had no fear or concern over the possibility of a negative outcome.

I then observed the seconds on the timer ticking by: 5...10...15...20. Then, just before it reached 25, I watched as the doctor used his hands to keep the lion's teeth from puncturing his neck. Finally, amidst alarms sounding and security people rushing forward to offer assistance, he calmly managed to pry the animal's vise-like mouth open.

I was certain this was all planned. Houdini also used to make his audience believe he was about to become victim to some incredible danger, only to emerge from his predicaments unscathed.

Once freed, Arno stepped back and patted the nose of the ferocious animal, which reluctantly backed up and once again sat lazily on the floor. It was as if it had enjoyed being in the spotlight.

Now it was time for the bear to have his chance at stardom. Arno now used his small stick to get the bear's attention, and it responded with several large roars. The huge animal, now standing upright, was then guided through several incredibly daring tricks.

(NOTE: I had seen other bears do these kinds of things in circuses throughout the world, but never by a monster this large.)

At this point, Arno decided to push the envelope further: suddenly, he dived at the animal's mid-section, knocking it to the floor. It was totally unexpected. To me, it was an amazing exhibition of sheer courage: he was actually wrestling with this fierce beast that towered over him by several feet and outweighed him by hundreds of pounds.

It did not take long for the bear to wrap its huge arms around Arno's waist and begin initiating what most wildlife experts would consider its most potent weapon: its ability to literally squeeze an opponent to death. But this was not to be the end of Dr. Arno. To everyone's relief, he yelled out a command and the huge bear immediately released him.

The monstrous animal then sedately walked back to its cage, followed by the lion. Never had any audience witnessed such training mastery.

Despite the audience's initial rage at Arno for putting his young son at such great risk, they had now begun to turn. I could hear scattered hand claps; just a smattering at first, but soon the smattering gained increasing momentum. Within seconds, it transitioned into a sustained round of applause that continued for three whole minutes.

Arno did not miss the opportunity to take a bow, and soon his son was standing by his side.

In the back of the auditorium, I could see three police officers. Obviously, several people in the audience, upon observing the youngster being ordered to put his head into the lion's mouth, had felt sufficiently alarmed to summon the police by dialing 911.

What followed was a sight no one would have ever expected that night. After just a few seconds of conferring with a small group at the back of the auditorium, the officers proceeded down the aisle and climbed up on the stage, then placed Dr. Arno in handcuffs.

What occurred next was the most surprising yet in a performance filled with surprising happenings.

All of a sudden, one of the officers walked over to the lion's cage and stunned the audience with what he did next.

With no hesitation, he led the huge cat back out onto the stage. This time, it was not Arno who was forcing the animal's mouth wide open—it was the police officer. The brave young man immediately responded by putting his own head inside and kept it there for a full 10 seconds.

By now, the audience did not know what to make of what they were witnessing. In fact, many in the crowd actually applauded when the officer removed his head, smiling and unscarred.

Strangely, I remember being as confused as everyone else. This all had to be a carefully choreographed stunt; in effect, a beautifully enacted hoax.

AND IT WAS.

The officers then introduced themselves as members of the college's faculty: professors of robotronics, the science of designing robots to replicate objects either living or extinct.

(NOTE: As indicated in other parts of this book, I prefer not to reveal the true identities of most of the people or institutions involved in my visions. To do so could cause undue attention prior to the completion of their work. In this situation, I decided not to identify the college or the real names of these professors. I will just refer to them as Doctors Fredericks and Bertram.)

Professor Fredericks, who appeared to be the spokesman, went on to explain that any living thing could now conceivably be replicated in robot form: in fact, in such intricate detail and so exacting in appearance, that only the closest of examinations could determine if they were or were not real. He further indicated that all such robotic forms could be controlled by either electronic or verbal voice commands.

With those comments completed, he walked over to the glass aviary and lifted the front panel so the birds could all fly free—which they did, fluttering and swerving all over the auditorium. Some flew up to the far reaches of the ceiling, while others chose to fly mere inches above the heads of the audience. Many made sounds, and a few actually came down to rest on the shoulders of some of the children in attendance.

After letting them loose, he then answered the question that must have been first and foremost in the minds of everyone in the audience: "Yes, each and every one of these birds are man made objects."

With that announcement, he took a small box out of his pocket and pushed a button. Amazingly, all of the birds flew back to their aviary, except for one which he plucked out of the air and carried over to a little girl so that she could stroke it and inspect it closely. The child caressed the bird gently.

Despite her delicate touch, the creature, which certainly looked real to me, squirmed and wiggled as if it was alive and fighting for its freedom.

Professor Fredericks pushed another button as he gently took the bird from the child, at which point several television screens came alive, displaying an enlarged image of the now-motionless creature. He then turned it over so that the cameras could clearly focus on its body as he peeled away the simulated feathers on its underside.

What was revealed to the shocked audience was a structure complete with a mini circuit board not unlike what one might expect to find inside a digitally controlled small model drone or airplane.

After laying it aside, he signaled for Dr. Arno to lead the huge bear, lion and tiger back to the center of the stage.

As they walked behind him, I kept thinking there was no way these animals were robots. The birds, perhaps, but these beasts, never. Their strides, head movements, and occasional sounds convinced me that all three had to be the real thing.

I soon realized even my trained eye could be fooled.

With great flourishes, both professors shouted out loud voice commands. To my utter amazement, all of the animals suddenly became motionless. The audience gasped.

At that point, Professor Fredericks went behind each one and carefully manipulated some instruments to allow for the individual removal of the outer coverings of their heads.

Under each one was an ingenious combination of circuits, microchips, wheels, cogs, and even miniature speakers—all beautifully united to produce a sense of reality beyond belief.

What particularly impressed the audience was the instrumentation that controlled the robotic workings of the lion's head and mouth. To accommodate their curiosity, the other professor (the one I call Bertram) pressed a few buttons and the ferocious mouth once again repeated its terrifying roar.

It was then that Professor Fredericks began to discuss the intricate steps taken to give the robots their appearance as genuine animals. He emphasized the substantial use of real leather, fur, imported feathers, and glass eyes.

He then segued into a question-and-answer session that evolved into a discussion of the incredible capabilities of advanced robotronics, from manufacturing applications, to travel, to robotic surgery, and to people-less armies.

Fredericks' passion for the unlimited use of robotronics was probably best personified in what he said next.

"Human lives will never again have to be put at risk in warfare. In fact, there will come a time in our scientific maturity where it will be almost impossible to distinguish between a robot and a real person."

It was then that Dr. Arno quietly brought his young son back out onto the stage. The audience broke out into a sustained three minutes of applause.

Then, he walked behind the child and, with a grand gesture—almost like a magician concluding a perceived miracle—lifted the incredibly realistic outer covering of the boy's head.

To the total astonishment of everyone (including myself), the child was not a child at all—he was a robot.

This was another startling and unexpected shock in what had already been a mind boggling series of shocks. Just a short while earlier, the audience was not only convinced this was a real youngster, but that his head might be bitten off by a lion.

Without a doubt, what I had witnessed was not only the coming of age of unlimited use of robotronic technology, but also one of the greatest thrill shows I have ever seen.

Then it all ended in a flash.

I was back in the wings of the theater in eastern Long Island, awaiting my introduction to perform. However, my mind was spinning with thoughts of what I had just witnessed. It was as if this incredible vision had a deeper meaning. As it turned out, I was to devote many hours considering its future impact on society.

As for my performance, I was soon able to clear my head so as to utilize my perceptive abilities to their maximum potential. Best of all, the audience had no idea what I had just experienced.

As I stood there thanking them for their applause, an intriguing thought entered my mind: would there someday be a man-made creation that could tune in and perceive people's thoughts? Possibly even a robotic Kreskin?

VISION No. 23

The Sea and Its Secrets Beckon to Me

———— ⚭ ————

I have always been fascinated by our planet's oceans. Many times I have stood at the water's edge, watching the sun sink behind a distant horizon. I would stare at the earth's curvature, wondering what went through the minds of ancient mariners as they sailed into a sea that appeared to drop off to nowhere. During such occasions, I would even ponder what lingers beneath its mysterious surface.

My next vision offered an opportunity to find out.

One of the blessings of having a modicum of success is that I receive invitations to appear at a wide assortment of venues. I have entertained in huge theaters, intimate nightclubs and college lecture halls, even in sports arenas, but few things give me greater pleasure than appearing on cruise ships. Somehow being at sea sets you apart from the problems, troubles and distractions that are easily left behind once you set sail.

These kinds of floating appearances also enable me to temporarily avoid dealing with airports, gloomy hotel rooms, and substantial amounts of fast food. Furthermore, they also provide an opportunity for me to get closer to my audiences by allowing me to occasionally lecture on various topics. These include my six-decade career, the many celebrities I have known and worked with, my outlook on the world, and a wide variety of additional other subjects.

There are others who lecture, often guest experts on various subjects. Their list of topics includes everything from geography and history to legends and mysteries of the sea. One subject that usually draws the largest audiences is the lost city of Atlantis.

Probably what perpetuates the fascination is the speculation regarding what part of the ocean hides the ruins of this legendary advanced civilization; most often suggested are locations off the coast of the Bahamas, or in the waters near Athens, or even somewhere off the tip of Spain.

Still more debated is the question of whether Atlantis ever existed at all. Most scholars believe that Atlantis (which is Greek for "island of Atlas") is only a fictional place mentioned in Plato's dialogues *Timaeus* and *Critias,* which were written around 360 BC; but I have listened to many guest lecturers who insisted the fabled city was not a fable at all.

Their rationale? Most asserted that Atlantis was a massive island-continent that actually did sink into the depths of the ocean. To document their contention, they would present their own version of evidence, much of which consisted of copies of old charts, photos of odd rock formations, huge shadow images taken from satellites in space, and images provided by remotely operated deep water exploration vehicles.

As convincing as these presentations often were (and regardless of how much the Atlantis devotees enjoyed hearing about them), they generally were not enough to tip the scales in favor of proving that the fabled city was truly real. Why?

The generally accepted belief is that there is not enough concrete evidence the fabled city ever existed, as the naysayers feel they have yet to see or hear anything that really constitutes a "smoking gun," or the kind of evidence that would stand up to rigorous scientific study.

This chasm in beliefs presents a major problem for Atlantis advocates. They simply are not able to present either the necessary artifacts or tangible proof to make their case. In fact, what they consider acceptable evidence often presents more questions than answers.

Most of these onboard discussions kindle spirited discussions. Fortunately, (usually close to meal time), they wind down with handshakes and their participants moving on to the ship's dining room, or one of the many diverse restaurants.

But on at least one occasion, the topic refused to disappear from the forefront of my thinking—to the extent that it may very well have been the catalyst for one of the strangest of all of my visions.

Often, when one of these happenings occurs (as I have mentioned before), I have an unmistakable sense of not feeling quite well, occasionally even slightly dizzy. Such a feeling often serves as a valuable precursor of what is about to take place.

This feeling came upon me in my stateroom immediately after one of the Atlantis discussions. It was approximately 4:00 p.m. (8 bells, in nautical time). I was sitting down, preparing to watch the ship's network of programs on television. It was at that exact moment that the on switch for my own special visions took hold.

In a flash, I was transported to an entirely different location.

But not to any destination on land: this one was still on a boat of some kind, but hardly a luxury liner. Gone was the rich carpeting under my feet. Gone were the polished brass doorknobs. Gone was the teak wood paneling. There definitely were no fancy trimmings.

In fact, where I now found myself immediately told me that this vessel was all business and no play, a craft built for something special. My intuitive guess was that its main purpose was ocean exploration.

In fact, the specific room I had been transported to was a large enclosed area filled with instruments of all sizes and shapes.

Fortunately, there was no great mystery as to what year I had been carried to; on the wall, almost hidden by what appeared to be hundreds of controls, buttons and dials, was an electronic international clock and calendar. It confirmed my suspicions. Once again, I had jumped substantially into the future, on this occasion to the month and year of April 2021.

I also noticed uniformed male and female crew members seated in front of a large bank of monitors not unlike what one might expect to see at NASA. Their screens were filled with all kinds of scientific data, including what appeared to be depth readings and various underwater images. What I was also "picking up" was a strong mood of pent-up excitement among these people.

Turning around, I could see the area in which I had arrived was adjacent to the ship's bridge. Directly in my line of vision were what appeared to be the people running the operation.

They definitely were not kids right out of college; from what I could determine, their ages varied from the mid 40s to the late 60s. They all had their own responsibilities, some preoccupied with maintaining the vessel's course, while others were manning the many computer monitors and related instruments. Regardless, they all maintained constant communication with each other whenever necessary. As usual, my overwhelming sense of curiosity took over.

Being in my usual spirit-like state, I could move around, observe, and listen to everything without anyone being aware of my presence. It appeared obvious that even the people running the show were exhibiting signs of excitement.

I was certain my initial intuition was correct. Something extremely positive had revved these people up. Everyone was either shaking hands or hugging. I had to know what it was.

Fortunately, I did not have to remain in the dark too long. The person in charge, whom I will call him Dr. Benson Shaw (not his real name), raised his hands and called for everyone's attention.

He then immediately ended my speculation as to where we were. In doing so, he confirmed what probably everyone knew (except me): we were hundreds of miles due east of Cuba in international waters.

The announcement of the ship's location struck a bell with me, because the combination of Cuba and underwater exploration signaled a memory of something I had read in 2012.

It seems there had been at least one other substantial archeological expedition not too far from Cuba; however, it was closer to the coast. At the time, the team's findings had surprised many in the scientific community. Why?

They had photographed underwater structures that appeared to be man made; some vaguely resembling pyramids, and even actual buildings. Still, this was not considered definitive enough to generate extensive excitement from true scholars; many felt that what had been discovered might only be natural configurations formed by underwater currents, rock slides, or even upheavals caused by earthquakes.

But that was 2012. I had now been transported into the future, to the year 2020. So I wondered, could all this hugging and shaking hands be due to what the people on this expedition had discovered? Was this craft sitting on top of an extension of the findings from the 2012 expedition? I was to learn that the answer was probably no.

It seems we were much farther away from Cuba than this earlier expedition had been, and in significantly deeper water.

So what was causing so much excitement among everyone on board this craft? Dr. Benson Shaw provided a partial answer. After he pressed a few keys on his computer's keyboard, several large monitors came alive amid cheers and even some applause.

Their screens were suddenly filled with incredible images of underwater structures that definitely did not appear primitive. What I (and everyone else) was looking at had to have been built by people with an advanced knowledge of architecture.

After a brief few minutes, Dr. Benson Shaw turned off the images.

Then, his voice almost cracking with emotion, he issued an order to be implemented as soon as possible. I remember him saying, "People, what you are looking at is real. Now we will be going down to gather proof of our findings." More cheers followed.

The words "going down" particularly caught my attention. I was thinking how much easier it probably would be exploring the ocean bottom in this year 2020.

I recalled that in 2012 filmmaker James Cameron had descended deep into the Mariana Trench in the Pacific Ocean, a depth of approximately 35,236 feet. It was hailed as a magnificent technological achievement. The word "magnificent" was appropriate, not least because the device he used to achieve this feat was what he called "the Magnificent Lime-Green Machine." It enabled him to not only personally observe what up to then, had been unexplored depths, but to also secure and retrieve objects of interest. A huge step forward.

Now, almost a decade into the future, it was safe to assume the submersibles on board this ship could substantially exceed Cameron's achievements. I felt like cheering as well.

At this point, I must explain that my presence on board this vessel was not a one-day experience. As fate would have it, it seemed that I remained there for a lengthy period of time, likely weeks. Extended stays during my visions were not unusual, and made little difference because I always returned at approximately the same time I left.

Fortunately, when I was later mysteriously returned to my cruise ship, I made sure that neither the extended nature of this absence nor the events I had witnessed would be forgotten through a combination of my enhanced memory and of course, my detailed notes.

(NOTE: Memory optimization is a skill I take great pride in. It is a subject I have talked and written about throughout the years. I have used it to remember names of whole groups of people in audiences and in lecturing on mnemonics (memory as it relates to the training of the mind). Consequently, this is an ability that has served me well in being able to recall much of what I have seen or heard during these experiences.)

You may also wonder how I could possibly have no sense of time or the actual duration of my visions. There is no simple answer to this question. When I am in a spirit state, the time of day has little meaning. I have no physical form. I have no needs. I feel neither cold nor warmth. A week can be like a day. A day can be like an hour. An hour like a minute. A minute like a second. I just exist wherever I am transported. Still, I listen. I observe. I learn.

Furthermore, for whatever duration of time I am there, it is always in their time—never in my own. What is even more incredible is that when my visions are over and I am transported back to wherever I was taken from, the hands on my watch indicate that no more than seconds have passed since the moment I left. In effect, very little measurable time has gone by. Such was the case with this vision. I certainly listened, observed, and learned.

Using these basic abilities and my growing familiarity with the changing moods of everyone onboard, it was easy to note that they were becoming more and more upbeat as the days passed. Laughter and smiles seemed to increase as time went on.

There was rarely any of the grumbling or complaining one usually encounters on a ship. Absent was the griping about the food or long hours. It was almost as if the crew and the research staff were struggling to contain not only their sense of excitement, but also their anticipation of some very positive happening.

Fortunately, their wait for that special event was about to end. It came out of the blue. Early one morning, Dr. Benson Shaw requested an ABES (all but emergency staff) meeting on the main deck. Needless to say, the effect of this announcement was like a starter pistol kicking off the beginning of an important race. There was an immediate scramble to obtain a favorable spot close to the makeshift platform he preferred to use when addressing staff and crew.

Everyone was fully expecting the news to be good. If they had any doubts, the look on his face dispelled all of their concerns. They knew that what he was about to say was exactly what they had been waiting to hear. I remember his words: "Ladies and gentlemen, we did it."

I am sure few, if any, listening to his remarks will ever forget the emotion he displayed in making his statement. It was enough to cause even me to wonder if we were all to suddenly become part of a historic event.

The answer was a profound YES!

What he confirmed was not the discovery of Atlantis. No. It was something far more important, and far more historic.

Dr. Benson Shaw was announcing the discovery of a massive undersea city. Miles long. Well below the 35,000-foot depth Cameron reached in 2012. And while that in itself would easily qualify as an amazing achievement, I soon realized just how significant an accomplishment this really was.

What had been discovered was a whole new civilization. An ancient society whose tantalizing relics indicated capabilities far in advance of those exhibited by any previous early civilization above or below the ocean.

I remember wondering what the news of this discovery would mean to the outside scientific community. From my point of view, it seemed highly unlikely that any of them would have expected such a monumental announcement to come from an expedition such as this. Of course, Dr. Benson Shaw, himself, consistently displayed a look of unflagging confidence. He knew something they did not—yet.

Dr. Shaw then confirmed that for the past few weeks, he had been in constant communication with several of the world's leading research centers. Not only had he been sending them a steady stream of photographs of the rather modern-looking structures he had discovered, but he had also forwarded a generous sampling of carefully extracted pieces of artifacts for purposes of chronological dating.

At this point, I was watching the expressions of everyone around me. And for good reason. The tension on the deck had been mounting, and it became evident that the repressed exhilaration of everyone onboard was about to burst forth (which, from my point of view, was way overdue).

Their emotions had been held in check for weeks, but now Dr. Benson's Shaw's words had unlocked their sense of contained joy. Suddenly, unbridled cheers and applause were gaining momentum, to the degree that even I got caught up in the mounting enthusiasm.

Still, I wanted to hear and understand everything Dr. Benson Shaw was saying. It was not easy.

Even though a restored sense of order had been accomplished, I now found it difficult to follow his presentation. He was beginning to use a considerable amount of technical language to explain the complexities of what had been accomplished; perfect for most of the researchers, but difficult for me, whose knowledge of oceanic archeology was limited to the basic science I had been taught in college.

Fortunately, not everything sailed over my head. Particularly the name of a famous place he kept referring to over and over: Mesopotamia. I remembered it as the world's oldest civilization, which I later was able to confirm as having existed from approximately 6600 BC to 3500 BC.

But Dr. Shaw's news was to take on even greater importance. The data received from the research centers was now confirming that their analysis of his many photographs and samples indicated this newly discovered underwater civilization could possibly be at least 15,000 years old. If such was the case, it would dramatically pre-date the existence of any other known early civilizations, including those that had their beginnings in China, Egypt and Peru.

But his presentation was to include still more surprises. In fact, what happened next turned the cheers and applause into wild shouts of praise and approval. Why?

Because, almost as if he was a magician, Dr. Benson Shaw whisked off the blankets that covered two of three tanks standing nearby. Each was filled with salt water, and the contents were now completely visible to everyone.

As it turned out, there was good reason for the startled reaction.

Although the first tank contained several objects of interest, the second held a huge piece of gold that caught everyone's attention.

Yes, gold. And quite a chunk of it.

What they were seeing was a massive nugget magnificently reflecting the limited light beaming through the nearest porthole.

Its resulting sheen made it appear as if it had been cut out of a mine mere hours ago instead of being plucked from the depths of the ocean two weeks earlier. In fact, it resembled the biggest nugget in the world, one that I had once seen on display at the Golden Nugget Hotel in Las Vegas. The only difference was that this nugget seemed larger.

Dr. Benson Shaw, noting the group's fascination with the gold, did not want their attention to go far adrift from the real bounty of this expedition: the discovery of a lost civilization. Consequentially, he quickly re-covered the tank holding the nugget and then called their attention to the first tank, which contained a number of other objects.

In doing so, he reminded everyone in attendance that this was not a hunt seeking pirate's booty. Absolutely not.

From Dr. Benson's Shaw's point of view, the presence of a substantially large piece of gold presented an important find, but in this early stage of exploration he was not able to ascertain whether it had been part of some large undersea vein or possibly a possession belonging to someone who lived in one of these mysterious structures. That would be something that might possibly be determined in the weeks and months ahead.

It was obvious he wanted to keep the incredible importance of the discovery of a 15,000-year-old civilization clearly in focus, and that while the nugget obviously was worth a fortune, it paled in comparison to the significance of the actual artifacts demonstrating the capabilities of the people who had been part of this civilization.

He quickly pointed out that this other tank held the artifacts that would constitute the necessary proof of its existence.

There were three artifacts in the tank.

Although they were still sitting in seawater to protect their delicate state, images of them suddenly appeared large and clear on the several monitors around the room. Dr. Shaw then underscored the necessity of maintaining them in seawater (something of which the majority of researchers in the room were well aware).

However, I personally found much of what he was now saying to be welcome information. He pointed out that such ancient artifacts tend to be extremely fragile, to the point that once they are lifted out of the water, they begin to degrade rapidly. Iron, for instance, can corrode so quickly that it not only can first become too hot to touch, but may soon crack into pieces from the internal pressure generated by chemical change. He added that the same is also true for wooden objects, which will often split and collapse immediately after being removed from water.

Dr. Benson Shaw then began to discuss each of the artifacts individually.

He pointed to the first one, still in good enough condition for him (and the on-shore researchers) to have determined to be an ancient padlock. Not just an ordinary padlock, but one of a rather complex nature. He indicated that it had been made of a processed hard metal and, although more than 15,000 years old, it displayed all the ingenuity of a lock made in the middle part of the 20th century.

I remember thinking, "What? Did I hear that correctly? Did he say it displayed the integrity of a lock made as recently as the last century?"

Indeed, he did.

Furthermore, Dr. Benson Shaw explained that this conclusion was confirmed by utilizing certain advanced radiocarbon dating technology, which indicated that, although the objects had the chemical and metallic characteristics of having been created in the 20th century, the results spoke more to the strength and quality of their construction. He also indicated that upon further treatment and restoration, they probably would display a potential for durability and reliability comparable to most locks of the same specifications available in 2020.

He then called everyone's attention to the next object, which he identified as some kind of musical instrument. It was approximately the size of a guitar. Beneath all the undersea life encrusted on its surface, there appeared to be numerous buttons and levers, most of which seemed to be there to control the nature of its sounds and volume.

Dr. Benson Shaw even jokingly mentioned his early college days, when he played with a small band, adding that he hoped to safely restore the instrument to a condition where he might use it as the centerpiece to resurrect his old group. If so, they would probably be justified in calling themselves The Relics.

The third object was larger than the first two and appeared to be some kind of miniature fireplace or oven. Dr. Benson Shaw pointed out that this was particularly noteworthy as it not only seemed to utilize a modern-day type of bolt, but here, too, its metal and construction was far advanced from what anyone might expect from a piece that was 15,000 years old.

But this raised a question: why was it found in a climate that should not have required artificial heat, found buried beneath the sea in a tropical zone?

Dr. Benson Shaw then emphasized that there were many more such objects that were not yet in a condition suitable for display; in fact, most were in various stages of protective treatment.

You might wonder, as I did, why some of the researchers onboard had not been aware that unusual items were being retrieved from the ocean's bottom. Actually, the almost secret hauling to the surface of undersea objects is common on research vessels, particularly in waters rumored to be the burial grounds of hundreds of ships that sailed from the Caribbean to countries like France, Spain, and England. In fact, such items are usually covered with seaweed and sea urchins when they are raised from the ocean's floor, making them mostly unidentifiable at the outset.

At this point, Dr. Benson Shaw agreed to take questions from his fellow researchers and the ship's crew. The first was the most important, at least from my point of view. How did such an advanced civilization get "swallowed up" by the sea?

Dr. Shaw offered up a broad explanation, which he stressed was based partly on facts at hand and partly on speculation. His best guess was that 15,000 years ago, this civilization probably existed in one of two locations, either on the coast of Central America or on the coast of Eastern Africa. He further speculated that the climate then likely was far different from what is it today.

Instead of the tropical zone that now blankets both of those continents, it probably was much colder and more oppressive. If so, that would explain the miniature oven found amidst its ruins. Storms might have been rampant. Days might have been shorter, and life as we know it today might have been far different.

At this point, I remember thinking that the big questions still remained unanswered. Why and how this civilization came to be?

Rather than address this mystery, Dr. Benson Shaw continued on the topic of its demise. He pointed out that, despite the high level of imagination and intellect of its peoples, the downfall of the civilization was probably due to the cruelty of nature's attacks.

He went on to stress that the planet at that time might have been under constant bombardment by meteors and affected by solar storms. This could have caused earthquakes that would have spawned super-tsunamis with waves as high as mountains that might have been more than capable of sweeping over any early communities and wiping away all traces of their existence.

There were several other questions from the group, then he posed one of his own: "Why had no one asked about the third tank that still stood covered by a blanket?"

Frankly, I had wondered about it. In fact, my eyes had never left it. But up to now, it had seemed as if not a single person had shared my curiosity. That was about to change.

I remember how his sudden inquiry caught the group by surprise. Almost in unison, all eyes turned to the tank and then back to Dr. Benson Shaw.

Within seconds, a frenzy of requests arose from his audience. They wanted to know what was hidden in the covered tank—and they wanted to know immediately.

Dr. Benson Shaw smugly smiled, and stated that what he was about to reveal was likely to change their perception not only of the true capabilities of early man, but of how much further advanced they really were.

With those remarks, he once again took the stance of a magician about to demonstrate the impossible.

In dramatic fashion, he began to count. One... two...

And then it happened. That strange feeling began to overwhelm my senses. My initial reaction was, "No, no, not now!" But to no avail.

Even as I felt myself being extracted from my surroundings, I could faintly hear him say the word "Three!" and then I could hear nothing further. The curtain had been drawn on another of my visions. Just like that, I had been transported away from an important time in our future.

Nevertheless, I was back in my cabin. All around me were the creature comforts of a cruise ship, a far different environment from the one I had just left.

Back? Yes.

Safe? Yes.

Angry? Yes.

Inside of me was a genuine sense of resentment. I kept thinking, "Not fair, not fair." I had spent the equivalent of several weeks on that vessel, and now I was to be deprived of learning what might have been its most important discovery. Every part of me wanted to witness what Dr. Benson Shaw was about to reveal. I deplored the possibility of never knowing what was inside that third tank.

I sat quietly for the next few moments, waiting for my feelings to transform into an inner calm. Of course, eventually they did: they had to, and for a number of reasons.

First and foremost, I knew I had been present at a time of great discovery, a privilege granted to few other humans. Yet, I will always wonder what I would have seen if I wasn't brought back at the count of three?

But, controlling emotions is what I have always taught, what I have always practiced, and what I have always believed to be a necessity. If ever there was an emotion that needed to be held in check, it is anger.

Nevertheless, I decided to wait a few days before making my customary notes. Somehow, I still hoped it might be possible to "will" myself back, not only to that destiny-bound boat, but to the point from which I had been withdrawn.

I should emphasize, there had been occasions in the past when I had been able to mentally transform myself to another place and another time; not for the lengthy periods as in these sudden unscheduled visions, but briefly, and with only minimal success. However, on this occasion, success in returning to that boat was to elude me completely.

After numerous attempts, I had to reconcile with the fact that I was to remain but an invisible witness to a cliffhanger, one that will take many years to be resolved.

The one note I wrote that evening was as follows:

"In the year 2020, a whole new civilization will be discovered that is far more advanced than the world ever thought possible. At that time, an undersea archeologist, to whom I have given the name Dr. Benson Shaw, will make known exactly what the full extent of this civilization's level of advancement was. That point will come when he lifts a blanket from the final of three tanks. My fondest hope is that I am in the front seat to watch it happen."

I put my notes away and checked my watch. It was now time for the ship's evening meal. Suddenly, I felt hunger. Not just a slight twinge of hunger, but a strong need to eat a massive meal.

(NOTE: Day after day, in my invisible spirit-like state, I watched Dr. Benson's Shaw's crew eat without having any sense of needing sustenance for myself. But that was then—and this was now.)

I entered the dining room knowing exactly what I craved the most; believe it or not, it was seafood—lobster and everything that went with it.

Frankly, my manners must have flown out the window, because I ate with a reckless abandon. And rightly so. The meal was memorable.

But it could hardly compare with what was to follow.

I noticed that the occupant of the next table had been watching me from the moment I sat down. As a performer on a cruise ship, it was not unusual to be stared at from time to time, particularly on this occasion, when my table manners were far from what they might have been. But I sensed this was different.

My first inclination was that possibly I had previously crossed paths with this person who stared with such intensity. Certainly over the years, I have participated in enough meet-and-greet sessions for an occasional face to have slipped beneath my personal radar screen. Therefore, I let my curiously dictate my actions. I simply leaned over, excused myself, and asked if we had ever met.

He smiled and apologized for his staring, it was just that he was a long-time admirer of The Amazing Kreskin and had a message he must deliver to me.

As is the case of any performer, I always like to hear words of praise. But a message? What was that all about?

At this point, my intuitive senses were telling me that there was something about him that cried out for my immediate attention. Nevertheless, I thought this "message" business was part of some joke.

So I decided to play along. Naturally, I asked what is his message was. He responded with just six additional words. "The dark will precede the light."

I looked straight at his face, expecting to see some indication of a smile or possibly some further explanation, but his expression remained unchanged. It was at that moment I realized he was serious.

Without saying anything more, he stood up, shook my hand and left. I was practically speechless. He simply opened the door leading to the deck and walked out into the night.

Something very strange had occurred; in fact, it was sufficient for me to immediately leave my seat at the table and follow him.

But to no avail. Suddenly, he was nowhere in sight.

Incredibly, as far as I could see, the deck was empty. How could someone vanish so quickly? I had only been about 20 feet behind him.

It was then that I wondered if I had not finally made contact with a live messenger from the mysterious forces that have been directing my visions over the years.

As events turned out, the answer was a definite yes.

(NOTE: The proof of that conclusion was justified by the two visions that followed this strange meeting.)

Actually, months went by after that bizarre cruise ship encounter; all the while, I kept thinking about the six words he had spoken before he vanished, "The darkness will precede the light."

VISION NO. 24

The Dark

———◦❦◦———

I was in the process of returning from several important meetings in New Orleans. My intention was to drive to Tampa and then catch a flight back home in two days. As I obviously had time to spare, I decided to travel along scenic U.S. Route 90, which would take me through Biloxi, Mississippi.

It was late in the afternoon, and the weather was clear and sunny. However, according to the weather forecast, an approaching front was bringing with it the possibility of fog. As a resident of New Jersey, a state filled with industrial plants emitting tons of dark fumes, the onset of fog was commonplace to me.

I had long ago learned the scientific explanation for what was in that kind of fog. It was made up of large clouds often bearing contaminants in water droplets suspended close to the ground. "Contaminants" being the key word. With that in mind, I never forgot that on rare occasions, fog could be deadly.

As an entertainer known for working with the mysterious and unknown, I knew that fog could also be an ally, which is why I would often welcome it as the ideal scene-setter for a Kreskin performance.

It is interesting how fog can mean different things to different people. It is fascinating to many, frightening to some, and comforting to others.

Over the years, I have witnessed fog in its vast array of impressive forms. Slithering above and below massive bridges, dipping mysteriously between endless peaks and valleys, eerily shrouding farmhouses, barns and silos, or just hovering in one particular place and stubbornly refusing to move on.

That is when it can become dangerous and potentially deadly, because when it stops and lingers in one place, it can "draw in" all the poisons around it, sometimes resulting in a horrific amount of destruction.

Considering the vision I am about to relate, it is probably appropriate to touch upon several instances where the refusal of a dense fog to move on caused death, destruction, and considerable heartache.

One such occurrence was on Tuesday, November 28, 1939, during a prolonged and unusual cold spell in St. Louis, Missouri.

It was on that date that a meteorological temperature inversion trapped the accumulated emissions from the soft coal burned by the city's residents for warmth and power. What followed was unlike anything the people there had ever encountered, a thick black cloud of smoke so dark, so dense, and so frightening that November 28, 1939 became permanently known as "Black Tuesday."

Those who remembered the fateful occurrence referred to it as, "the day the sun didn't shine." As it turned out, it could have been called "the long black week," as the fog lasted a full nine days.

Then there was the fog that settled in Donora, Pennsylvania, on Tuesday, October 26, 1948. Although hydrogen fluoride and sulphur dioxide emissions from a local steel mill and zinc works frequently enshrouded the town, the weather phenomenon known as a temperature inversion made the situation substantially worse on that day.

It was a horror that left 20 people dead. By the following Monday, the fog's lethal mix had also sickened almost 7,000 men, women and children — exactly half the town's population. It has been called "America's Worst Air Pollution Disaster," and is said to be one of the reasons for the passage of the Clean Air Act in 1963.

In effect, the fog suffocated the life out of the community. Donora today stands nearly empty. Its single gasoline station, lone dollar store, and row of abandoned storefronts paint a far different picture from the Donora that existed before the fog, as do the now- shuttered steel mills and coke plants that line the Monongahela River.

Still other instances have demonstrated the deadly potential of fog. One very memorable lethal example occurred in London, England, on December 5, 1952 and lasted for five hateful days.

London, of course, was quite used to fogs, even dangerous ones, but this one turned out to be a ruthless killer. It quickly thickened to a poisonous brew so dense that residents in the Isle of Dogs area of the city reported they were unable to see their feet when they walked. By the time it lifted on December 9, it had taken the lives of 12,000 people.

The most likely guess as to its cause was that the pre-winter conditions had necessitated the burning of extra coal to fight the oppressive chill. What resulted was excessive smoke laced with sulphur dioxide, nitrogen oxides, and soot from the low-grade coal that smothered London in a black cloud of near-total darkness. To this day, it is still considered the worst pollution disaster in British history.

Allow me to take you back to my decision to drive through Biloxi, Mississippi.

As I indicated, it had been a bright, super-warm afternoon in southern Mississippi.

Still, the forecast of possible fog and a growing fatigue caused me to do the sensible thing and spend the night in this, one of my favorite destinations. I hardly wanted to keep driving and find myself on the state's fog-bound, high-speed Route 10.

Actually, there were many reasons for me to be fond of Biloxi. It offered a wonderful array of sugar-white beaches, a wide choice of restaurants and, by virtue of its many casinos, an abundance of star-studded entertainment.

I was pleased to find it once again looking in pristine condition. Not so, nine years earlier – immediately after August 28, 2005. That was when it sustained a powerful hit from Hurricane Katrina.

The storm's Category 4 winds pushed a huge tidal wave (which some estimated as reaching 40 feet in height) surging from the furious Gulf of Mexico over the beach and across U.S. 90. It then went about its work, destroying everything in its path for several miles inland.

Happily, the former antebellum homes along the water have been rebuilt, the sugar-white beaches are again beyond compare, and the casinos have been rebuilt and even expanded. To me, finding this treasured spot as I had always remembered it was a welcome sight for a tired driver.

Still, what I wanted most was a good night's rest. Fortunately, I knew exactly the place. It was a tiny inn across from the Gulf with nice rooms, a decent kitchen, and good service. I definitely wanted to avoid the party atmosphere of many of the nearby casinos. I realized that I knew too many people not to be immediately recognized upon entering any of the gambling palaces, and I wanted to avoid countless handshakes, backstage visits with performers, and overeating in the fancy restaurants. I simply wanted peace and quiet.

That was a far cry from what I was to experience that night. I remember checking into my usual room. It was as I had remembered: comfortable, with a clear view of the Gulf, and with a small terrace. In essence, it was perfect. My next goal was a hot meal delivered up to my room, a glass of wine, and a comfortable chair in which to relax.

By the time I had finished dinner, it was just beginning to get dark. While Biloxi is hardly Las Vegas, the lights from its various casinos come alive as soon as the sun sinks. I remember watching their reflections on the water. As I did, I commended myself on my decision to stop here for the night.

The darkness had obscured approaching storm clouds. In fact, I was startled by the sounds of thunder reverberating from the waters of the Gulf of Mexico.

Next came sheets of rain. They were relentless and pelted my terrace. There even seemed to be hail mixed in. The storm must have continued for several hours. I remember lying in bed listening as its rhythmic sound beat against the small table outside. Finally, it stopped.

It was now 3:00 a.m. Curious, I got up and walked over to the terrace doors.

Instead of observing the lights of the casinos in the distance, I was greeted by sheer blackness caused by a thick fog every bit as dense as anything I had experienced in New Jersey.

I absolutely could not see farther than the blurred images of occasional car lights on the highway mere feet from the front of the inn. Still, as I was only half awake, I felt my curiosity had been sated.

Usually, I found fog conducive to sleep, but not this time. The sheer blackness beyond my room's terrace served as a curious reminder of the words uttered by the stranger on the cruise ship: "The dark will precede the light."

Could the thick, almost-impenetrable fog outside be the "dark" he had referred to? In looking back, I almost wish it had been.

Why? Because what I was to experience was far worse.

Somewhere in the hours between 3:00 and 5:00 a.m., I sat up, suddenly. I was beginning to once again sense the approach of what I suspected might be another mystical trip. By now, I knew this feeling well. This time, I actually felt a desire to fight it with all my inner strength. But as hard as I tried, I realized it would be a losing battle.

Consequently, rather than resist, I decided to simply relax and let fate take over.

It required mere seconds (possibly even nanoseconds) for me to find myself standing in total darkness in the middle of a street in some strange city. Inwardly, I joked, thinking that if I had a dog, I would probably say, "Toto, I don't think we're in Biloxi anymore."

However, even though the darkness was pitch black, I was to later learn that I had arrived at my destination in what was actually the middle of the day. Furthermore, this was not a strange city at all.

Looking around me, I was familiar enough with my surroundings to realize I was in the New York metropolitan area. But where? I was engulfed in a fog so thick I could barely make out my hands when my arms were extended.

But my inability to see was only part of the problem. As people passed me by, I could hear them coughing. It was obvious that the fog contained contaminants that probably were potentially sickening.

I realized that in my present spirit-like state I would be in no physical danger, but I had to get to some indoor site where there might be light and more information what year I had been transported to and the extent of this fog. Fortunately, I was able to spot a light in the entrance of a nearby building. It was faint and blurred at best, but still, it was enough to enable me to make my way to the doorway.

Once inside, I realized exactly where I was: standing in the vestibule of the Prentice Hall building at 5th Avenue in New York City. I considered this a great stroke of luck, because I knew the broadcast studios of the Fox network were just a few short blocks away. If anybody would have a handle on what was going on, they certainly would, but getting there would not be easy.

While the inside of the Prentice Hall building was well lit, outside it still resembled the middle of the night. I would need help. Once again, fate smiled on me. Almost as if my inner thoughts were being heard by unseen forces, help came into view.

I was able to make out the blurred images of two New York City police officers moving past me and heading straight to the door. Fortunately, they were both carrying heavy-duty flashlights. I simply trailed behind. I found myself practically walking in their footsteps, which were heading north on 6th avenue. The strategy proved a good one. In just minutes, I was entering the Fox studios on 48th street and 6th Avenue.

I had been here on many occasions, usually as a guest on one of their discussion shows. I had also been invited back for numerous New Year's Eve specials. My function? To provide live, on-the-air, exclusive "top of my head" predictions for the ensuing 12 months.

Let me again describe what a requested Kreskin prediction is (so as not to be confused with my visions). Often, as is the case with my guest appearances, I am asked to use my mental abilities to provide an instinctive perception of a future event. I receive many such requests—from individual hosts, guest panels, or groups of people at after-show meet-and-greet sessions.

However, before accommodating them, I try and emphasize (as I've indicated earlier in this book), that I am not Nostradamus: I neither use crystal balls, nor strange elixirs.

I am a mentalist, period.

I can only respond with what I instinctively feel, sense, and perceive as coming from my audiences.

My visions are a different story. These are occurrences to which I have in some manner (that I still do not understand) been allowed to be a witness. Consequently, I am much more confident that what I have been privileged to see will come true. That is why the accounts are here for you to read.

I realized this visit to the Fox studios was different. There would be no smiling producers waiting to greet me, none of the big-name reporters to visit for a quick hello. I was here under more somber circumstances, which, because of their nature, I suspected would leave me with few, if any, positive memories.

Except for one. I recall going directly inside to the broadcast facilities. Keep in mind, in my spirit-like state, I was totally invisible. I was free to head in any direction. As a result, I had little trouble finding my way to Fox's main newsroom.

Strangely, even though I was well aware that I probably was somewhere in the future, most things looked the same. In fact, other than some new wall coverings and studio decor, not too much of the physical layout had changed. I wondered about their well-known broadcast personnel, if there had been many changes.

Fortunately, according to some of the posters on display, many of the personalities I had grown to know and like were still around. But none were to be seen. I had to assume most of their programs had been preempted due to this incredible fog. Furthermore, I am sure many of them lived far enough away to preclude their making it to the studio. Nevertheless, I would have enjoyed seeing a few of these old friends.

I still hoped I could at least find a few. (And if I could, what would they look like?) With my curiosity further aroused, I had more reason than ever to determine exactly how many years into the future I had been led; particularly since up to now I was in the dark—literally.

Fortunately, I did not have to search for long. The answer was right there on a nearby desk calendar.

(NOTE: I realize that by now I should not be surprised as to where these sudden mysterious excursions take me. But admittedly, once again, I was shocked.)

Incredibly, I had been transported to April 2021, approximately seven years beyond my 2014 starting point. It was obvious I was in the midst of a serious situation. But I had to know just how serious.

Fortunately, one of the studios contained a large window that looked out on the street. It was part of a large set that allowed television viewers to look beyond the broadcasters and view the surrounding New York City neighborhood.

However, if I expected to see any daylight, it wasn't happening. Everything was still pitch black.

As I continued to explore the Fox studios, I remember how everyone around me seemed to be in motion. The place was in an obvious state of high alert, not the usual calm and orderly news organization I was used to seeing. I kept thinking, if ever there was a period when a little disorder was excusable, it was now.

I had to admire the many reporters firmly attached to their computer terminals. Their news-gathering instincts were in high gear. Their eyes were fixed on the contents of their screens, hoping for any kind of new data information. I had no doubt the personnel at other networks were equally as dedicated to obtaining additional information.

I certainly shared their curiosity. Inwardly and instinctively, I had little doubt that the rest of the United States was engulfed in the same terrible situation as New York City.

At that point, I remember recalling the fog tragedies in St. Louis, Donora and

London. I wondered how many men, women, and children of this 21st-century people had already been stricken by this hideous example of nature run amok. How many men, women and children had been made sick? How many lives had it prematurely ended?

I continued to move freely around the newsroom for what must have been several hours. Occasionally, I would stop and pay attention to the large TV screens. Most were broadcasting a parade of meteorologists and scientists, gathered remotely from wherever possible to provide opinions and expanded descriptions of this nightmare.

Then came the bulletin everyone was waiting for. Additional news was now feeding into the studios and going live on the air. It revealed the parts of the nation most severely affected by the fog. These included both coasts of the United States and certain areas in the Deep South. There were also reports that the fog's dense, dark clouds had penetrated hundreds of miles inland.

As if all of this was not dire enough, most experts stressed that there was no reason to believe these conditions would end soon.

This new information signaled a massive opening of floodgates of more expert opinion. Everyone now wanted to have their say. Screens throughout the studios were alive with talking heads. Not to be outdone, Fox had quickly arranged a pickup of the city's mayor, who was assuring everyone that shelters were being maintained for people trapped long distances from their homes and that emergency services were still functioning.

Of course, there were Congressmen, Senators and even the Vice President calling for investigations into the nation's weather reporting capabilities. As expected, there were also religious leaders of all denominations urging prayer, calm, and continued faith. These included a few apocalyptic preachers suggesting that this darkness might be a precursor to the world's end.

Some of the reports expounded on why the topography of some locations was more conducive to fog formation than others. They also indicated that these conditions could become particularly dangerous if fog lingered in one place for too long a period.

Of course, I knew this only too well. I realized that it was the contents of the water particles in the fog's mist that posed the greatest menace. They were the carriers of the toxic components that could possibly snuff out life.

There was still another piece of information that further alerted me to the danger New York City was facing: the city had entered its eleventh day of inundation. Based on all past history of deadly fogs, I knew this was the point at which it could become most lethal, virtually strangling the city's population with the poisonous content lingering in the droplets.

I recall thinking, "Oh my God."

By now, more data pertaining to additional parts of the United States was running across the bottom of the television screens. It seemed the fog had lingered for approximately the same amount of time in most of the other major cities in its path, cities like St. Louis, Seattle, Boise, Little Rock, Kansas City, Branson, Detroit, Harrisburg, Philadelphia, Charlotte, Atlantic City, and on and on. Very few areas had escaped its horror.

I remember thinking that the elected officials who were already calling for investigations into the lack of advance warning of this monster were well justified in their outrage. With few exceptions, various local, regional, state and national agencies had failed to provide any indication of the formation of this horrendous meteorological event.

Now everyone was hearing graphic descriptions of the resulting damage in both property and lives; millions of people throughout the world were getting a very strong message regarding its awful potential.

The stories being told were similar to those recounted by survivors of terrible tornados and earthquakes; they described cars piled up along roads, of people wandering aimlessly, and of the constant wail of sirens everywhere. Fortunately, there were some photos available that had been taken with cameras equipped to shoot in the dark.

During those grim hours in the Fox studios, I also remember watching an earlier broadcast of the President attempting to calm the nation.

Despite his insistence on patience, trust and confidence in the government, none of his comments seemed to ease the worries of the ordinary people who were featured in the follow-up interviews. I could even sense a tone of resentment and defiance in some of their remarks; the main emotion they displayed was disappointment.

Why? Because despite his words, there was no scientific resolution or possible ending in sight.

Nevertheless, people were doing their utmost to suppress panic. I could see that everyone working at Fox that day was a prime example of adapting to a bad set of circumstances. I learned that for the full period of unrelenting darkness, some members of their staff had remained at the broadcasting facility, using couches to sleep on and eating whatever food was available.

While the network's 6th Avenue location was the home of famous hotels, corporate headquarters of many of the world's most prestigious companies, New York's diamond district, and Radio City, it was not exactly a hub for convenience stores. Even if there had been such establishments nearby, chances are there would have been no employees on hand to assist customers.

So what could they do? I noted that the station had opened up its already hard hit vending and soda machines (as well as its supplies of cookies, crackers, and candies used for restocking). Management also asked employees who were able to return each day to bring extra food to help feed their coworkers.

(NOTE: I learned that, through this whole crisis, New York City's transit system had remained operational. Subways had been running, albeit on a substantially limited schedule, so passengers who were able to safely reach a designated train station were able to travel to various parts of the City's five boroughs. Unfortunately, two problems precluded it from being a means of dependable transportation: 1) Switching problems necessitated the designated stations having to be changed constantly; and 2) the incredible blackness represented a significant safety danger to anyone attempting to reach a station without a police officer to guide them.)

Fortunately, employees at Fox would not have to be deprived of their coffee. It seems a substantial mother lode of java had been found somewhere on the premises. Consequently, everyone around me had enough of the magical elixir to function at their normal high level of productivity so that their work continued.

The fog seemed relentless in its refusal to dissipate.

Once again, checking the various television monitors, I could see that fresh experts continued to be called upon to provide new perspectives on what was happening. Some were even accepting questions submitted by viewers.

Incidentally, even though many television and radio stations were still broadcasting, many were not. They had been knocked out of commission by vehicles crashing into telephone poles and towers, resulting in downed lines and other communication problems. In many instances, repair trucks either could not get through to make the necessary fixes or were not allowed on the unlit streets and highways. Surprisingly, there still appeared to be enough people with service to generate a substantial response to the programming.

Viewers were utilizing what I suspected was the 2021 version of mobile email. Their questions were literally streaming into the TV studios, including Fox's. I was able to read a few of them. One person wanted to know what the difference was between this dark black fog and the kind of fogs cities customarily experience, or whether this was possibly not a fog at all, but perhaps something far different.

The reply was that, despite how impossible this current blackness was to see through, what all of the affected areas were experiencing now was still definitely a fog, though certainly not the common kind people are used to. This one, of course, was much thicker and darker because of the soot and chemical content of the fine water crystals responsible for the fog's density.

While many such dense fogs cause considerable difficulty in range of vision (often limiting visibility to possibly no more than an arm's length), this one had produced sheer blackness.

This brought up the question of whether this fog could be classified as a pea souper, and the answer was that this monster might even be classified as a super pea souper.

The term had originated in London, which had long held a reputation for being frequently socked in by bouts of thick fog combined with coal dust and other pollutants. Another question pertained to the possibility of breaking up the fog with large amounts of water. The consensus was that substantial amounts of water deposited over most fog formations could conceivably break them up and make them dissipate. But this was not like most fogs.

With a fog of this density and wide range of coverage, authorities would have to almost dump a lake over most large cities. The subsequent amount of water would be hundreds of times greater than what is typically spread over the nation's largest forest fires.

The result would be massive flooding over cities and in the countryside, plus destruction of crops that would take years to restore. There would also be substantial damage to homes and other physical property. So, yes, water was a theoretical way to end the crisis, but in this case, it was not the answer.

I remember that the day had turned to evening, which meant it was prime time for the nation's airwaves to be handed over to the likes of its newscasters. I was sure that millions of Americans were waiting desperately for answers. This made me wonder how many of the top people from all of the important news centers, including CBS, NBC, and ABC, whom I knew in the present, were still around now, in 2021. Unfortunately, I was not destined to learn the answer. Why?

Because all of the main networks were posting on-screen notices indicating that the evening's regular programming had been cancelled so that ongoing coverage of the fog could continue.

The hours that followed provided more information from local stringers about the deadly consequences of the fog. I realized I had been sent here to witness all of this and someday tell about it. I wondered when I would be transported back to my original time.

These thoughts continued until about 5:00 a.m. It was then that the first statistics on loss of life began to emerge. Initial reports indicated approximate deaths had exceeded 40,000, with a caveat that this was only an early estimate. The total could be substantially revised upwards. Injuries were being reported in the over-100,000 range. With that awful news, I decided to move to the outdoors. I suddenly needed more space.

In my present state, I of course required no sleep, food or even that precious commodity–coffee. Although the thought of being able to enjoy a real cup of the stuff somehow seemed very appealing.

I walked out of the vestibule of the Fox studious greatly saddened by the news of all the fatalities. I am a Christian, but certainly far short of enough church visits to be held in the highest graces of my parish priest. Yet, when appropriate, I occasionally say a personal prayer whenever I believe such a prayer might be helpful.

This was such a time.

So there I was, standing on the gleaming pavement of New York City's 6th avenue, looking upward and quietly asking for the Almighty's intercession. By now, it was close to 6:00 a.m.

I just stared up into the darkness, hoping against hope that somehow, some way, my meager prayer might be heard. I remained there for over five minutes. As I looked around, I saw others actually down on their knees doing the same thing.

After a while, I lowered my head and started walking back to the building's entrance.

That was when I heard screams coming out of the darkness. People were suddenly racing past me shouting, laughing, smiling, and looking up into the blackness and opening umbrellas.

Yes, umbrellas.

It was not just raining. It was a deluge. Harder than any rainfall I could remember. Probably enough rain to end the fog. I inwardly said "Thank you," confident and comforted that millions of prayers had been answered.

It was at that point that I suddenly found myself transported out of the dawning of a more hopeful New York City back into the early morning light of my Biloxi hotel room.

Without hesitation, I immediately started making notes on the incredible vision I had just experienced. I wrote for a long while. In the midst of my attempting to record everything, I remembered the stranger I had met on the cruise ship and his parting words: "The darkness will precede the light."

I now wondered again what the significance of those words were.

VISION No. 25

The Light

A number of months had gone by. It had been a busy time for me, yet I still felt invigorated and was looking forward to bookings all the way through the month of February 2015.

One particular date jumped out at me. It was February 22, the birth date of possibly the greatest man in American history, George Washington. I have always been fascinated by the beginnings of our country, and particularly by our first President, and was now more so than ever. He was to play an important part in my next vision. In fact, it turned out to be more of an "epiphany" than just a vision. And what an epiphany it was.

But first, let me tell you a little more about this great man.

To be totally up front, I should let you know that I have always believed there was a spiritual connection between George Washington and the mystical powers that contributed to the creation of America.

I am also convinced that his role in America's birth and survival may have been guided and even protected by divine intervention. This is a contention that seems to be supported by historical events, testimony and documents, some even in the Library of Congress.

One such document pertains to Washington as a 23-year-old British officer during the Battle of Monongahela in the French and Indian War. The unrelentingly bloody fight eventually resulted in a stunning loss for the British, and even in the death of their leader, General Edward Braddock, and many of his officers.

But young Washington was not one of them. His survival amidst this brutal combat was to give birth to the legend that he could not be killed.

The validity of his invincibility was demonstrated in another violent two-hour skirmish in which everyone around him was falling like targets in a turkey shoot—

yet bullets whizzed past him. Owing to his height, Washington was a larger-than-life target; he was almost impossible to miss.

At the end of the raging conflict, he emerged unscathed. In fact, the only damage he sustained was a bullet hole in his hat and several others through his jacket—which served as dramatic reminders of his proximity to death.

Fifteen years after the battle, the great chief of the Indian tribes that had attacked him that day sought him out. Unfortunately, the name of this warrior-leader is lost in the archives of history. However, I was able to determine why he had devoted so much time to searching for Washington.

It seems this leader of the many tribes that had defeated the British wanted to meet George Washington to personally tell him of what he described as a miracle: the witnessing of a man who could not be killed.

Although their meeting was quite lengthy, what I am about to describe is more or less the heart of what he supposedly revealed to Washington. The great chief indicated he had traveled a great distance to meet the General George Washington personally. He detailed how, on the day of the attack, he instructed his warriors to take careful aim and make sure they hit the tall officer leading the fighting.

He told of how his warriors seldom missed their targets, emphasizing how they had little or no difficulty hitting Washington's subordinates, but shooting the brave young officer himself seemed impossible. No matter how true their aim, they were unsuccessful.

It is said that the chief told Washington of a sudden realization that his opponent was being shielded by a power mightier than any power he as a great chief possessed. He then ended their meeting by telling Washington he had come to pay homage to the man who was a particular favorite in heaven, a man who could not die in battle.

There is no record of how Washington reacted to this curious tale.

As strange as this story was, there is one substantially stranger, a ghost story of sorts. It tells of Washington's ability to return from the mysterious world of the dead.

The accounts describe a meeting between Washington and Civil War general George McClellan. It was during the year 1862, when, unbeknownst to McClellan, his plans for the defense of Washington, D.C., had been stolen by a traitor and given to the leaders of the southern forces.

It was at 2:00 a.m. on the third night after McClellan's arrival at his post in Washington when, weary over studying maps and reports of scouts, he collapsed into a deep sleep. It was about 10 minutes later when he found himself awakened by an authoritative voice that said:

"General McClellan, do you sleep at your post? Rouse you or, ere it can be prevented, the foe will be in Washington."

It is said he then saw a living map of America accompanied by the vague outline of a man. The map contained what appeared to be the complete pattern of the enemy's troops, invaluable information that would assure him an easy victory. But looking more carefully, he now saw the enemy occupying positions he intended to occupy.

It was at that moment the voice spoke to him again:

"General McClellan, you have been betrayed. And had not God willed otherwise, ere the sun of tomorrow had set, the confederate flag could have waved over the capital and your grave. But note what you see. Your time is short."

It was at that point that the light and glory shone more brightly on the figure near him. He raised his eyes until they looked directly into the face of George Washington, who then said:

"General McClellan, while yet in the flesh I beheld the birth of the American republic, it was indeed a hard and bloody one. But God's blessing was upon the nation, and, therefore, through this, her first great struggle for existence, he sustained her and with his mighty hand brought her out triumphantly.

"A century has not passed since then, and yet the child republic has taken a position of peer with nations whose pages of history extend for ages into the past. She has, since those dark days, by the favor of God, greatly prospered. And now, by very reason of this prosperity, has she been brought to her second great struggle.

"This is by far the most perilous ordeal she has to endure. Passing as she is from childhood to opening maturity, she is called on to accomplish that vast result, self-conquest—to learn that important lesson, self-control, that in the future will place her in the van of power and civilizations.

"But her mission will not then be finished, for, ere another century shall have gone by, the oppressors of the whole earth, hating and envying her exaltation, shall join themselves together and raise up their hands against her. But if she still be found worthy of her high calling, they shall be found discomfited, and then will be ended her third and last struggle for existence.

"Thenceforth shall the Republic go on, increasing in power and goodness, until her borders shall end only in the remotest corners of the earth, and the whole earth shall beneath her shadowing wing become a universal republic. Let her in her prosperity, however, remember the Lord her God; let her trust be always in Him, and she shall never be confounded."

It is said that Washington then raised his hand over McClellan's head in a blessing, after which the General awoke with a start and set forth immediately to thwart the enemy's plan. His subsequent action saved the nation's capital.

General McClellan told of this visit many times. In fact, one such account was concluded with these words:

"Verily, the works of God are above the understanding of man!"

Important!

What I have detailed here was printed in the *Evening Courier* of Portland, Maine on March 8, 1862, and was never repudiated by General McClellan.

There are many other examples of George Washington's extraordinary closeness to God, but I hope the inclusion of just these two happenings will be enough to convince you of his precious relationship with the Almighty, and his readiness to use it to go far beyond what has been commonly described in history books.

FAR, FAR BEYOND.

What follows is an account of my own incredible encounter with our first President, and why it was an epiphany.

Yes, it happened.

As I have already indicated, George Washington's birthday has always been special to me. His time, his feats, and his contributions to America were the foundation for my love of history. I was particularly fascinated by the accounts of his strong affinity to God.

I remember reading of his being stricken with smallpox while on a surveying assignment to Barbados in 1751. For any ordinary person, such an encounter should have cut his young life short, but Washington was hardly ordinary. It is said that in the midst of his life-and-death struggle, he heard a mysterious voice telling him he would be spared because of an important mission he must fulfill. Of course, we all know what that mission was.

(NOTE: The evidence of his battle with smallpox is visible in many portraits of Washington: close examination will reveal the disease's telltale pockmarks on his face. It is also important to keep in mind that he contracted the disease on a primitive island without any medical facilities during a time when smallpox was a ruthless killer. Yet a powerful force saved him, a force for which all of the millions of Americans who followed should be eternally grateful.)

Later, when I read of his middle-of-the-night visit to McClellan, I wondered, "Could this have been part of the mission Washington was told he must fulfill? Was he to become God's own special messenger?"

Although there have been many other sightings of the ghost of this great leader, I will never know all of the people he may have confronted during this nation's 200-plus-year history. What I can confirm is that I was to meet him, in a manner of speaking. It was a happening I will never forget.

This is how the fantastic event came about.

Actually, this strange day did not start well. I had taken a rather turbulent flight from Los Angeles back to New Jersey. It was five hours of being shaken and rattled, an experience that left my stomach in an unreceptive mood for a semi-stale sandwich and some nuts (even when served in first class). Nevertheless, we finally landed at Newark Airport.

As was often the case with these cross-country flights, I was immediately impressed with the marked contrast between sunny South California and the chilly Northeast. Earlier that day, the California sky had been blue, and balmy temperatures lingered in the comfortable 70s. Here, it was frigid.

However, everything soon became right again. Within 90 minutes, I was back in the den of my New Jersey home.

In fact, I remember how warm and comfortable it felt. I lost no time in seating myself in my favorite chair with the television turned on. I wanted to determine what was going on everywhere. It's funny how being confined in a jet plane for five and a half hours can give you a feeling of detachment from the real world.

Yes, they do have on-board TV monitors that rebroadcast day-old news. But that is exactly what it is: day-old news. I am curious by nature; I have to know what is going on as close to when it is happening as is possible.

So I simply sat back and closed my eyes and prepared to listen to the latest news. It took less than 30 minutes until I felt myself growing tired. Although I could only hear the anchorman's words, the name of our nation's capital was referenced several times: Washington...Washington ...Washington.

(NOTE: I realize your first inclination might be that my hearing those words might have set the stage for what was to follow. But I assure you it did not. Furthermore, I want to re- emphasize that what I was about to encounter was so much more than just a vision. It was to become an epiphany. So here it is, a journey never to be forgotten.)

It began with the customary strange feeling that precedes all my mystical transitions. Before I could give any thought as to how fast I was being catapulted to the location of my next destination, I was there.

But where, exactly, was "there"? Fortunately, the answer soon became obvious.

It was a vast green meadow surrounded by what appeared to be countless rows of headstones. However, this was not just any meadow. A weather-withered wooden sign told me I was standing in the midst of thousands of our honored dead in the hallowed fields of Valley Forge.

Later, in my notes, I indicated how that realization generated a feeling of stark loneliness.

It was near sunset, and even though there was still some daylight, there were no other human beings in sight. Consequently, this huge expanse bearing the remains of thousands of patriots seemed sadly forgotten.

I need to emphasize again that when caught up in a sudden excursion like this, my lack of a physical body does not allow for the carrying of writing materials, which is why, upon my return, I tried to expeditiously make notes of everything this revered individual had to say. What you are reading is the result of my determination to get it all down on paper, and to do so as quickly and as accurately as possible.

This had not been the case with General McClellan. He was very much alive at the time of his encounter with George Washington, and able to practically write down Washington's words as he spoke them (and, in doing so, capture the same style and syntax common in those revolutionary times).

My eyes were drawn to what was first a shadow, then unquestionably the figure of a man. I dared not hope, but then could not deny what I saw and felt.

Washington's ghost was coming toward me, coming ever nearer. I found it interesting how none of the artists who have painted his likeness really captured the full essence of this man. He seemed to project a stronger sense of confidence and inner power than has been depicted in even the paintings of Gilbert Stuart (who, incidentally, was not one of the General's fondest admirers).

What came next startled me. For the first time, I heard George Washington's voice. It was deep, resonant, dominant.

He told me that he was about to reveal information that I was to convey to as many people as would listen. I wondered what that meant.

Trepidation took over. What awful piece of news was he about to make known? What hopeless message of doom was he about to ask me to pass on to an already-nervous world? What end-of-our-time date was he about to reveal?

It was at that point that I remembered the accuracy of the predictions and information he had given to McClellan. They had been right on the mark. His revelations had saved the Union.

Therefore, I had to be mindful of the great importance of what he might predict. This was not Nostradamus speaking. This was not Edgar Cayce. This was the Father of Our Country, a unique prophet with a perception of the future that was potentially so much more important than what either of those other two seers could have ever revealed.

George Washington did not speak to me in ancient quatrains, or in a long-forgotten language. He did not lie on a bed and go into a trance. Despite the fact that his English was hardly modern, I had no difficulty understanding what he was saying.

I recall waiting for him to provide whatever fateful information he intended to disclose. I even recall a sense of fear and mentally bracing for what he would make known to me. Instead, I was in for a slight surprise.

He told me to look up at the birds flying freely above the treetops.

The birds? What was this all about? I was soon to realize that this would be part of his most profound promise.

He then remarked that from this present date, their peaceful flight would continue uninterrupted for 200 years. But then I wondered, what was the present date? In all my fascination with this great man, I had yet to identify the exact time in the future to which I had been transported.

But not to worry. It was almost as if he could read my thoughts.

He immediately identified the current year and date as July 4, 2176. Yes. I had been transported over 162 years.

He then said, "Come with me. There is a world beyond this sacred burial ground that is far advanced from what you have in the century from which you journeyed."

Suddenly, I was no longer in the Valley Forge cemetery. Instead, I was in the midst of a large city, staring at buildings that only faintly resembled the skyscrapers of 2015. It was all different. The vehicles in the street were different. The clothes people were wearing were different. Even the noises were different. Yet everything looked pristine, ultra modern and clean.

I was trying to think of how to react to what I was observing all around me. I recall saying something hardly worthy of the wonders I was seeing. All I could think of was that, fortunately, our country was intact and things seem to be going along fine.

Washington looked at me and replied, sadly, "Things are not going fine. Even on this day commemorating our quadricentennial celebration, war and killing are continuing throughout the planet."

I remember the word "killing" striking a note.

Killing? Even now, 400 years after the war for our nation's independence? Even now, 162 years after the mounting acts of terrorism that were threatening the world in 2015?

Washington could see I was very disappointed.

Then, almost as if to clarify his comments, I recall him saying, "Up until now, there were brief periods of peace. Times when America, being the kind of nation we are and always will be, continued to place itself in harm's way to help maintain these occasional stretches of relative calm.

"But the same basic issues of hatred remained constant elsewhere. Conflicts continued to re-ignite differences in religious philosophies, and demagogues continued to feed their thirst for more power. Nevertheless, within America, people will continue to live and prosper."

At that point, George Washington stated loudly and clearly, "There will be many positive changes that will have occurred."

Here are just a few (and I am listing them as best as I can recall):

1. Understanding and tolerance will again prevail in this nation.
2. Skin color will no longer be an issue in determining a person's fitness for a job.
3. A vast economic boom will elevate our standard of living to its greatest heights.

4. Much sickness and disease will be eliminated.

5. Crime, while it will still exist, will decrease substantially.

6. Lobbyists and corruption will be eliminated. Here, Washington made a point of adding that elected political figures will acquire such a complete understanding of the needs of their constituents that the profession of lobbying will tend to diminish remarkably, as will corruption. People of trust will tend to dominate the key positions in government.

The need for individual gun ownership will be greatly lessened. (This was another issue he wanted to clarify. Guns, when needed, will be in the hands of those who are guarding our nation's interest, the defenders of our country, and local, state and federal police to protect against crime and terrorism.

7. Our nation will again be the most respected and envied country in the world.

He then moved even closer and spoke of five more predictions he would make known to me only on the condition that they not be revealed until the year 2020. I readily agreed and then listened in fascination. What he told me was even more riveting than what he had already revealed. For the most part, it was not bad news; however, these additional revelations still left me somewhat shocked. I did vow not to reveal any of them before that date, and I will keep my promise.

I was hanging on to every word he said. My mind was alive with hundreds of questions, but I dared not interrupt him. Somehow I managed to manifest a sudden burst of courage, and heard myself asking George Washington one small question.

"Sir," I said, "I realize our current world will have to continue in the same dangerous climate that now exists, but will we always be the America that is the most desired, envied, and compassionate place to live in the whole world?"

For the first time, I noticed a fine smile become visible on his face. He looked at me squarely.

"My friend," he said, "Despite all of its continued challenges, the birds will continue to fly, and our flag will continue to be the greatest symbol of freedom and democracy that ever existed."

By now, it was evening, and he motioned for me to look up. There, shooting through the heavens were thousands of fireworks igniting on this 4th of July, the celebration of our nation's 400th birthday. In the background, I could hear strains of "America the Beautiful." It was stirring.

It was remarkable.

It was at that moment, almost as if on cue, that I was whisked away from the incredible vision of a future sky illuminated by our nation's flashing colors of red, white, and blue. Suddenly, I was back at my home in New Jersey.

As I sat there, still astounded by what I had seen and heard, I once again recalled the stranger I had met on the cruise ship, and his parting words: "The darkness will precede the light."

Now I wondered, had I just experienced the light?

But that was a question to ponder at another time. As for now, I felt filled with new hope for the future. Yes, the date July 4, 2176, was too far away to affect this current generation. But for our great, great grandchildren, and their children, it suggested that, as a nation, we would survive all of our challenges and problems.

And even though I would not be part of this new and stronger America, my mind and body were filled with elation.

I remember calling down to my secretary, Carol, to make reservations at the most expensive restaurant in town, and to make sure they had a fine vintage champagne.

I also remember her puzzled reply: "What are we celebrating?"

The only response I could think of was: "AMERICA."

Epilogue

My Dear Reader,

I owe it to you to share that I wrote most of this book a year ago. Yet, many of these visions have been with me for a great many years.

I weighed whether or not I should make the visions within this book public. I wonder as I look over these writings if it would have been wiser to release my visions earlier. Not that it would have changed history—I can't assume that kind of influence—but it may have caused some to readjust their perspective of what was coming up in the future or perhaps prepare for it.

I don't even know how or why these visions came to me, nor do I have any real knowledge of what will reach fruition and come true. But understand that what I have exposed to you had deep impact on me when I experienced them and has not left me in the ensuing months.

I also want you to know that my commentary and reflections on outer space are more than simple musings about the possibilities of extraterrestrial intelligence. You see, I believe that we have the wisdom and will attain the know-how, with the right dedication, to prevent the ending of our world. I don't think any scientist would deny that someday, certainly not in the near future, the sun will no longer warm life on this planet and that the ability to exist on this planet will diminish. It has happened to other terrestrial bodies as astronomers have commented.

But, if and when we return to our space research, as inspired by Armstrong and all of his fellow collaborators, there may be time to find other areas on which man can move and live and continue human life as we see here on Earth. Indeed it is my conviction that this will be the ultimate aim and achievement of space research.

Kreskin Bio

With a showman's flair, a comedian's wit, and the capacities of a bona fide Mentalist or thought reader, The Amazing Kreskin has, for six decades, dramatized the unique facets of the human mind. His very name has become an integral part of pop culture throughout the world.

Through the past fifty years Kreskin has had a television series, his own board game by Milton Bradley, nineteen published books, and a major motion picture inspired by his work.

In the 1970's Kreskin headlined his own television series for five seasons called 'The Amazing World of Kreskin.' Since the series, Kreskin has traveled over 3 million miles performing his unique brand of Mentalism in front of millions. Kreskin was also a fan favorite guest on Johnny Carson, Regis Philbin, David Letterman, and most recently, Howard Stern and Jimmy Fallon.

In 2009, actor and producer Tom Hanks released the feature film 'The Great Buck Howard,' starring Tom Hanks and John Malkovich. It is announced at the end of the movie that the inspiration for the main character is The Amazing Kreskin, the character played by John Malkovich.

In the 2010 movie, 'Dinner for Schmucks,' the character played by Zach Galifianakis has as his hero and influence The Amazing Kreskin, which further exemplifies the wide scope of Kreskin's exposure and impact.

2014 brought a whole new realm to Kreskin's arsenal when he mentally trained three up and coming boxers to victory, one of whom was Heather 'The Heat' Hardy. Kreskin parlayed his new 'sports psychologist' moniker into the world of Manny Pacquiao, helping him to victory against Chris Algieri. In May 2015, going one step further, Kreskin predicted the winner of the now legendary Mayweather Vs. Pacquiao fight, in which he successfully predicted a Floyd Mayweather win.

Through the years, Kreskin has received continued international recognition for extraordinary predictions about world affairs and occasionally sports, from the prediction regarding the U.S. Presidential Election in 2012 that was broadcast on 'Late Night with Jimmy Fallon' to his 2013 Super Bowl prediction which Kreskin predicted on FOX television.